DISASTERS

Natural and Man-Made Catastrophes
Through the Centuries

DISASTERS

Natural and Man-Made Catastrophes Through the Centuries

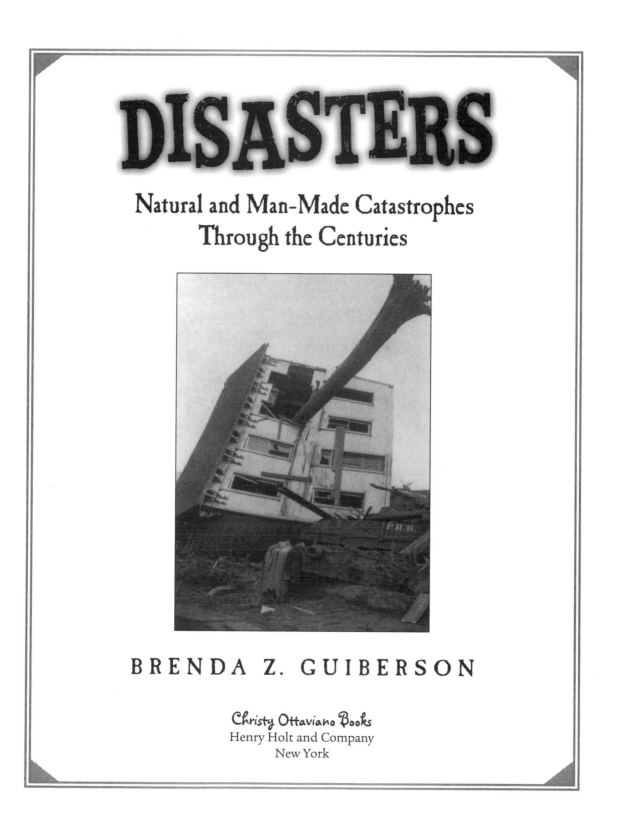

BRENDA Z. GUIBERSON

Christy Ottaviano Books
Henry Holt and Company
New York

Thanks to Christy Ottaviano, Eve Adler,
and all those at Holt who brought
their expertise to the many layers of this book.

Art Credits
All illustrations and photographs by Brenda Z. Guiberson except for the following, which are used with permission:
4: Courtesy of National Library of Medicine and WHO; title p., 7, 12, 17, 18, 38, 44, 53, 59, 64, 73, 84, 88, 115, 127, 140, 156, 158: Courtesy of Library of Congress; 24, 28, 36: Courtesy of Chicago Historical Society; 1, 51, 55, 66, 122, 146, 151, 160, 180: Courtesy of NOAA; 92, 93, 98: Courtesy of International Ladies Garment Workers Union Archives, Kheel Center, Cornell University; 117: Courtesy of National Archives at New York; 128: Courtesy of National Museum of Health and Medicine, Armed Forces Institute of Pathology, Washington, D.C. (Reeve 14682); 133: Courtesy of University of Washington Libraries, Special Collections, UW1538; 168, 174: Courtesy of Marco Garcia; 192: Courtesy of Jocelyn Augustino/FEMA; 198, 204: Courtesy of Captain Jason P. Smith, United States Marine Corps; 202: Courtesy of Andrea Booher/FEMA

Henry Holt and Company, LLC
Publishers since 1866
175 Fifth Avenue
New York, New York 10010
www.HenryHoltKids.com

Henry Holt® is a registered trademark of Henry Holt and Company, LLC.
Copyright © 2010 by Brenda Z. Guiberson
All rights reserved.
Distributed in Canada by H. B. Fenn and Company Ltd.

Library of Congress Cataloging-in-Publication Data
Guiberson, Brenda Z.
Disasters : natural and man-made catastrophes through the centuries / Brenda Z. Guiberson.
p.   cm.
"Christy Ottaviano Books."
Includes bibliographical references.
ISBN 978-0-8050-8170-1
1. Natural disasters.   2. Disasters.   I. Title.
GB5014.G83 2010
904—dc22
                                                    2009018908

First edition—2010/Design by Elynn Cohen
Printed in September 2010 in the United States of America by R. R. Donnelley & Sons Company, Harrisonburg, Virginia

10 9 8 7 6 5 4 3 2

For Laurie Dunn,
who brought so much passion and
intrigue to these pages

CONTENTS

DISASTERS

Natural and Man-Made Catastrophes
Through the Centuries

Introduction

*D*rops of water glistening on a spiderweb are a delight. A stream of water gushing through a forest is a wonder. But a 40-foot surge of water created by a colossal earthquake is a disaster. Nature in big doses changes our world.

This book travels through times and places that were drowned by water, consumed by fire, buried by dirt, or shaken by the earth itself. It includes intimate quotes and stories from survivors, rescuers, profiteers, and leaders. It teems with details of Indian tribes destroyed by disease, soldiers sickened in trenches, overconfident ship passengers stopped by an iceberg, and young children overworked and underpaid in dusty, dangerous sweatshops.

Disasters provoke questions. What really caused the dust clouds of the 1930s that buried farms in several states? How could Mrs. O'Leary and her cow get blamed for the fire that burned the city known fondly as the "Queen of the West"? How did a virus travel around the world in 1918 and kill more people than World War I, World War II, the Korean War, and the Vietnam War combined? How could an entire city drown after a hurricane that was not as strong as predicted? How could a tsunami catch some by surprise, but not everyone?

Questions need answers. Did you know that water can be more precious than gold? That wetlands are needed to protect coastal lands from waves that can reach as high as 100 feet? That plowing up the grass is a recipe for huge dust storms? That animals detect natural disasters more quickly than humans? That a virus is a parasite, always looking for a host?

Disasters come with warnings, and this book exposes them. Beware of floodplains, fault lines, and Hurricane Alley. Watch out for icebergs, sneezes, and toxic molds. Sometimes it is dangerous to open the refrigerator. Sometimes the best action is to head for the hills.

Nature will always shake, sizzle, gush, and wallop. It has the strength to destroy but also the systems to protect and restore. There is much to be learned from a close look at past disasters. The clues can lead to wiser choices for living in the natural world.

CHAPTER ONE

Smallpox

The Parasitic Horror

A Tricky Virus

Starting in the early 1600s, a great disaster struck Native Americans living across the land that would become the United States and Canada. Their population was drastically reduced, from 20 million to less than one million. Ninety-five percent dead, with some tribes extinct! One cause of this great tragedy was a microbe so small that 50,000 of them could fit on the period at the end of this sentence.

This horror was the smallpox virus. As a parasite, it must continually find a new human host or it will die. For thousands of years, throughout Asia, Europe, and Africa, among emperors, kings, and poor folk too, smallpox made people so sick that they often died. The virus survived by traveling to new victims in a sneeze, a cough, or the pus of an oozing rash. Millions of contagious microbes lingered in scabs that fell, after

Smallpox, the variola virus, can cover the body and be transmitted through contact with an infected person or with objects that have touched the infected person.

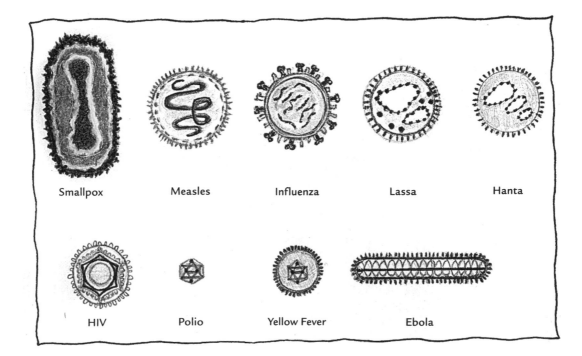

Smallpox   Measles   Influenza   Lassa   Hanta

HIV   Polio   Yellow Fever   Ebola

four or five weeks, from the dried-up rash of survivors. Blankets and clothing could remain contagious for months.

Over the centuries, Old World populations built up defenses against smallpox. One in three people with the disease died. Lucky people who did not get sick passed on this natural resistance to their children. The survivors ended up with an army of defensive microbes in their bodies to protect them from another infection. But children were always born who had yet to catch it. Then a coughing visitor sick with smallpox would arrive. A new epidemic would sweep through the crowds until the tiny microbe ran out of hosts.

But smallpox was unknown in North America. Explorers, settlers, slaves, and missionaries from the Old World were

The smallpox virus, variola, is the largest virus. Poliovirus is the smallest. Each virus has a different lifestyle that we must understand in order to prevent or cure it.

the visitors who transported it there. Unseen and uninvited, this parasite played a huge role in the shaping of the United States.

New World, No Resistance

It is the early 1600s along the coast of Massachusetts. Native Americans meet European fishermen who have come ashore for freshwater. Soon a strange sickness with fiery pain and oozing rashes sweeps through the tribe. Traditional medicines offer no relief.

A mother cradles her feverish child, who has red spots in his mouth and a rash on his skin. The child coughs and sends a spray of saliva into the air, each droplet containing thousands of a tiny virus that no one can see. The mother inhales some into her nose.

Quickly, the virus drills into a cell of her body. Once inside, the parasite stops the cell from doing its normal work and turns it into a smallpox factory. Thousands upon thousands of new viruses are reproduced until—*poof!*—the cell explodes into a shower of hundreds of thousands of new microbes. The pox spreads to lymph nodes and travels through the bloodstream. Eventually, it sickens the lungs, spleen, eyes, liver—so many important parts of the body.

After a week, the mother is bedridden with severe aches, nausea, and high fever. The child dies. Mourners bring food and carefully remove the child in his soiled blanket. Without knowing it, they become new hosts for the parasitic virus.

LANDING OF THE PILGRIMS AT PLYMOUTH 11ᵗʰ DEC. 1620.

Soon a rash breaks out on the mother's skin. When the blisters ooze with pus, it smells like rotting flesh. No one comes to help her. Too many are dead or dying, and the rest have fled in a panic to another village. They have become the visitors who continue the chain of infection. Any survivors will have deep pockmarks on their face, and some will be blind after four weeks of terrible sickness.

Since no Native Americans have been ill with this virus before, or with other illnesses introduced by Europeans, none have the defensive microbes left over from the sickness.

This 1620 Plymouth scene shows Pilgrims unloading items from the Mayflower *as a lone Native American watches.*

Meeting no resistance, the parasite invades and overwhelms most of them.

When the Pilgrims arrive on the *Mayflower* in 1620, they find the deserted village of Patuxet. The land is already cleared and ready to be planted, but there are no people, only graves and scattered bones. Meeting no resistance, the Pilgrims move in and call it Plymouth.

More Than One Way to View an Epidemic

Shiploads of Puritans arrived in Massachusetts in 1630. In 1633 another smallpox epidemic raged. William Bradford, governor of the Plymouth colony, wrote about the death toll in one of the tribes, stating that more than 950 of 1,000 died, "and many of them did rott above ground for want of buriall."

In the Plymouth colony there were 20 deaths from smallpox. Most of the adults had been exposed to the disease before. The parasite mainly infected children under 12, who did not yet have immunity.

Because the Indians were dying in such great numbers, some colonists thought the disease was caused by God, for their benefit. Increase Mather, a Puritan clergyman in Boston, wrote, "The Indians began to be quarrelsome concerning the bounds of the land they had sold to the English, but God ended the controversy by sending the smallpox amongst the Indians . . . who were before that exceeding numerous. Whole towns of them were swept away, in some of them not so much as one Soul escaping the destruction."

Others, however, used direct observation to learn about the disease. They realized that smallpox spread when a sick person came into contact with a healthy person. As a harbor town, Boston had a steady supply of newcomers, and some arrived sick. In 1647, the city authorities decided to isolate them with a quarantine. Ships were not allowed to dock until infected passengers died and were buried at sea, or until the last crusty scabs of the pox fell off, which could take four or five weeks.

This was not the end of smallpox, however. Ships held in a long quarantine did not make money, so many devious captains found ways to slip through. The city of Boston had five major smallpox epidemics in the 1600s, even after the practice of quarantining had begun. And disease continued to invade new tribes as trade and exploration expanded to new areas of the country. Millions died all the way to the West Coast, leaving desperate survivors with a loss of confidence in their culture and their gods. Some Native Americans had been enslaved by Europeans looking for workers, but so many of them died that a trade opened up to bring slaves from Africa.

The Power of Information

Increase Mather had a son named Cotton. In 1677–78, when he was 15, Cotton survived a smallpox epidemic. Later he became a Puritan clergyman like his father. In 1706 he was given an African slave, and Cotton Mather learned something new: "Enquiring of my Negro-Man Onesimus, who is a pretty intelligent fellow, whether he ever had ye smallpox, he answered Yes and No; and then told me that he had undergone an operation, which had given him something of ye smallpox, and would forever preserve him from it, adding . . . whoever had ye courage to use it was forever free from ye fear of the contagion."

This operation was called inoculation. Mather read that it had also been used successfully in the Ottoman Empire. Matter was removed from a smallpox pustule on a mildly sick person and then inserted into needle scratches on the arm of a healthy person. At the scratch site, a single pockmark erupted. The body would make microbes to attack the virus and then protect the inoculated from getting full-blown smallpox.

When the next smallpox epidemic broke out in 1721, Mather urged all 10 of Boston's doctors to consider this procedure. But like many devout Christians, they believed that smallpox was God's punishment for sin and they should not interfere. Also they were afraid of the surgery, and with good reason. Inoculated people sometimes got a severe case of smallpox or developed an infection. One in 50 died. All inoculated patients had to be isolated for three or four weeks because during that time they were contagious.

One doctor, Zabdiel Boylston, used a sharp toothpick and a quill to inoculate his six-year-old son and two slaves. All three were mildly sick and then immune. Many people in Boston were outraged and afraid. An angry crowd threatened to hang Boylston, and someone threw a bomb through Mather's window that failed to explode. It carried a note: "Cotton Mather, you dog. Damn you! I'll inoculate you with this, with a pox to you!"

Privately, Mather had his son Samuel inoculated.

Dr. Boylston continued also, and 280 more people were inoculated. Only six of them (about 2 percent) died. Throughout Boston (population around 11,000) about 5,800 got smallpox and 844 (about 15 percent) died.

Enough people heard about this success that inoculation was used in other cities. After his son died of smallpox in 1736, Benjamin Franklin supported it in his newspaper, the *Pennsylvania Gazette*. Many people traveled great distances to get inoculated, but the numbers were not high enough to slow down the disease. The procedure was very expensive, and people had to take off weeks from work. Only wealthy families could afford it; inoculation became an event where they all remained together for the entire isolation period. Benjamin Franklin thought that the poor should not be the main victims of the disease. In 1774, while he was living in England, he helped to start the Society for the Inoculation of the Poor.

Biological Warfare

Native Americans were left out of the first inoculation programs. But even more tragic, they sometimes became targets of biological warfare, deliberate plans to infect them with the smallpox virus.

In 1763, France and England were at war for control of North America. Some Native American tribes under Chief Pontiac, an Ottawa leader, tried to drive the British out of tribal areas. In May, they surrounded the British stronghold of Fort Pitt in Pennsylvania.

After a month of siege, the British devised a plot.

Sir Jeffery Amherst, commander in chief, knew that the Native Americans were susceptible to smallpox. He wrote to Colonel Henry Bouquet asking, "Could it not be contrived to Send the Smallpox among those Disaffected Tribes of Indians?"

The colonel responded, "I will try to inocculate the Indians with some Blankets that may fall in their hands, taking care however not to get the disease myself."

Amherst replied, "You will Do well

Mah-to-toh-pa (Four Bears) was chief of the Mandan tribe, which almost became extinct as Europeans spread out across North America bringing new diseases and aggressively seeking land.

to try to Innoculate the Indians by means of Blanketts as well as to try Every other method that can serve to Extirpate this Execrable Race."

Earlier, when two Native American chiefs were invited to visit the British camp, William Trent, a trader, wrote this in his diary: "Out of our regard for [the chiefs] we gave them two Blankets and an Handkerchief out of the Small Pox Hospital. I hope it will have the desired effect."

The chain of infection cannot be followed with certainty, but the tribes soon suffered another terrible epidemic.

Smallpox and the American Revolution

The American Revolution was fought while smallpox raged. During these years of war, between 1775 and 1783, more than 150,000 colonists in Canada and the United States died. About 25,000 were killed during battles with the British. Most of the others died of smallpox.

George Washington survived smallpox when he was 19 and had many pox scars on his face from the ordeal. He learned of the success of inoculation but for a long time resisted it for his troops because they would have to be quarantined afterward and would be unable to fight for weeks. And there was always a risk the disease could spread in spite of all precautions.

In April 1775, after the first battle of the American Revolution, the British retreated to Boston, where yet another smallpox epidemic was raging. The disease was killing Bostonians, but British soldiers had been inoculated and were protected.

The colonial militia camped outside the city and tried to cut off any supplies that might come to the British. But Washington feared a possible plot to spread smallpox to his troops. On November 27, 1775, he wrote to Congress that the British General "has ordered 300 inhabitants of Boston to Point Shirley in destitute condition. I am under dreadful apprehensions of their communicating the Smallpox as it is rife in Boston." Washington ordered sick people coming from Boston to stay away, and the army remained pox-free.

Meanwhile, other troops marched up to Quebec to try and win control of this key location from the British. In December 1775, Caleb Haskell, a fife player, wrote, "The smallpox is all around us." Later he became ill. "No bed to lie on; no medicine to take; troubled much with a sore throat." In the history of this disease, smallpox often determined who won the military battle. In this case, the British suffered far fewer losses than the colonial troops, and Quebec remained in the hands of the British. It did not become part of the colonies.

In 1776, the British gave up Boston. Fearing smallpox contamination on sheets and towels left behind, Washington at first only allowed his soldiers who had smallpox scars to enter the city.

Finally in January 1777, General Washington decided to inoculate his troops. He hoped "that in a short space of time we shall have an Army not subject to this the greatest of all calamities that can befall it." During the harsh winter of 1778 at Valley Forge, it was discovered that about 4,000 soldiers still had not been inoculated. There were more surgeries, and many soldiers spent the winter in bed cared for by others who were immune. After this, the number of smallpox outbreaks dropped considerably in the troops. The American Revolution ended successfully for the colonists. Native American cultures across North America, however, continued to lose battles with smallpox.

The Power of Observation and the Face of a Milkmaid

Smallpox belongs to a family of poxviruses that affect every species that gathers in swarms, herds, flocks, and crowds. There are mousepox, monkeypox, skunkpox, pigpox, gerbilpox, sealpox, canarypox, penguinpox, dolphinpox, grasshopperpox (six kinds), turkeypox, beetlepox, and butterflypox, just to name a few. But it is cowpox that plays an amazing role in the history of smallpox.

In the 1790s, while Europe was at war with France, a country doctor in England named Edward Jenner noticed that milkmaids always had clear, smooth skin. When he investigated, he discoverd that during the smallpox epidemic of 1778, they did not get sick. And a song in country folklore indicated that milkmaids had a long history of no smallpox.

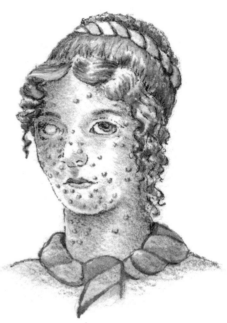

Smallpox survivors were left with deep, pitted scars. Some were blind. Native Americans called the sickness "rotting face." But Edward Jenner noticed that milkmaids had no scars, and, he wondered, why didn't they get smallpox?

Where are you going, my pretty maid?
I'm going a-milkin', sir, she said.
What is your father, my pretty maid?
My father's a farmer, sir, she said.
What is your fortune, my pretty maid?
My face is my fortune, sir, she said.

Jenner investigated and learned that milkmaids got cowpox on their hands after milking a cow with pox on its udders. Cowpox was a mild disease that was never deadly and left no pockmarks. Could they be getting immunity to smallpox without actually getting the disease?

Jenner took pus from the pox of milkmaid Sarah Nelmes, made two small scratches on a boy's arm, and inserted the pus into the cuts. Cowpox could not be transmitted from person to person, so no quarantine was necessary. Jenner wrote that "on the ninth day, [the boy] became a little chilly, lost his appetite, and had a slight headache. Spent the night with some degree of restlessness, but on the day following he was perfectly well." Jenner then did a very risky thing. He tried to give the boy smallpox through inoculation. Fortunately, the boy was immune.

Jenner wrote a book about this procedure. Matter taken from the cow he called *vaccine*, which comes from the Latin for "obtained from a cow." The procedure was called vaccination. In the United States, a Harvard doctor named Benjamin Waterhouse read the book. He tried the procedure on his five-year-old son and six others. Finding success, he

The Cow Pock — or — the Wonderful Effects of the New Inoculation! — Vide. the Publications of ye Anti Vaccine Society.

wrote to President Thomas Jefferson about this incredible discovery.

Once again, people responded with fear and religious objections. Some thought it was unnatural to interfere with the will of God. Some worried that characteristics of cows might pop out of their bodies. One English doctor claimed to know a vaccinated girl who "coughed like a cow, and had grown hairy over her body."

But Thomas Jefferson supported the new procedure. He invited Native Americans to the White House to be vaccinated.

This 1802 painting by James Gillray illustrates a common fear that vaccination could cause cow hair and cow parts to grow on human bodies.

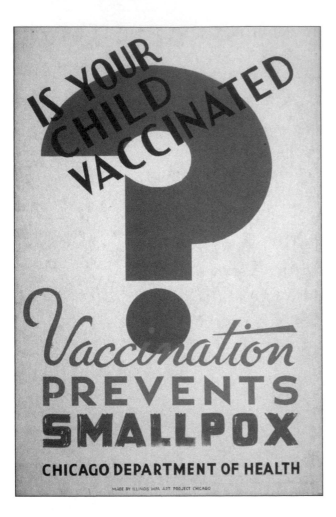

This 1930s poster from the Chicago Department of Health was part of the worldwide effort to eliminate smallpox.

He also sent supplies with the explorers Meriwether Lewis and William Clark and gave them instructions to vaccinate the various tribes they met. However, many Native Americans were suspicious and refused. An epidemic in 1837 almost wiped out the entire Mandan tribe along the Missouri River. All across the West, Indians continued to die in great numbers with devastating effects on tribal cultures from the Mississippi Valley to the Great Plains, and the Pacific Northwest.

The Death of Smallpox

The vaccine did not reach everyone. In the 1900s, an estimated 300 million people worldwide died of smallpox. This was more than the number of people who died during wartime in the twentieth century, from AIDS, and the 1918 flu pandemic combined.

But the most amazing part of the smallpox story also occurred in the 1900s. Smallpox became the only natural disease to be totally eliminated. The last known case in the world occurred in 1977; the smallpox parasite was finally contained and could find no more hosts.

This happened for several reasons. The vaccine had continued to work and had been given to millions around the world, including newborn babies and anyone who had contact with smallpox victims. Also, smallpox did not remain in the body of survivors or hide in any nonhuman host. And the virus did not mutate, or change. It always acted the same, so the body's immune response could fight effectively.

Most doctors today have never seen a patient with smallpox. Well-guarded frozen samples of the virus are kept in Atlanta, Georgia, and in Koltsovo, Russia, for scientific study. There are reports that other samples also exist, but this is not known for sure. Everyone hopes that this tiny parasite will never again reappear to find a new host.

CHAPTER TWO

The Great Chicago Fire

October 8, 1871

The Early Days of Checagou

Chicago burned on October 8, 1871, in what the local newspaper called "a calamity without parallel in the world's history." But before the city could burn, they had to build it. And how and where they built it had a great deal to do with the incredible size of the fire.

Chicago rose up over windy swamplands where the Chicago River flows into Lake Michigan. Before European settlers arrived, Native American tribes lived in the area and called it Checagou, which means "stinking-smelling place" or "wild

onion." Here they followed the only ancient trade route where they could carry, or portage, their birchbark canoes over the land route that linked the Great Lakes with the Mississippi River system.

Wars were fought over this valuable crossing, and tribal boundaries were defined by it. European explorers, trappers, fur traders, and missionaries found the shortcut and used it too. The muddy link became known as the Chicago Portage, and both France and England considered digging out a canal to allow boats to pass through. But on prairies that flooded

"Checagou" just starting out in 1820.

whenever it rained, no one stayed long, and a canal was not built.

Finally around 1780, a fur trader, named Jean Baptiste Point du Sable, built a log house at the mouth of the river. This black man from the present-day island of Haiti became the first permanent Chicago settler.

Indian Removal

After the American Revolution, more and more settlers came to the Great Lakes area, cleared out timber, and hunted wild animals. Native Americans, weakened by smallpox epidemics and other hardships, saw their way of life disappearing and fought back. Several tribes were defeated in 1794 by General "Mad Anthony" Wayne and 2,500 men at the Battle of Fallen Timbers. A treaty signed the next year opened new tribal areas for U.S. expansion, including "Land Six Miles Square at the mouth of the Chickago River emptying into the southwest end of Lake Michigan." This was the real estate deal that turned Checagou into Chicago.

Native Americans continued to try to reclaim the land. Black Hawk, a Sauk leader, had signed a treaty in 1804 but soon resisted as the government and settlers continued to force his people from their land. This led to Black Hawk's defeat in a war in 1832. The Illinois militia was called in to remove the Indians, and Abraham Lincoln, a recent settler, served as a captain. On orders from President Andrew Jackson, Black Hawk was taken to Washington, D.C. There, he said, "I touched goose quill to the treaty—not knowing, however, that, by that act, I consented to give away my village. Had that been explained to me, I should have opposed it, and never would have signed their treaty, as my recent conduct will clearly prove."

President Jackson had written to Congress that "the destiny of the Indians . . . depends upon their entire and speedy migration to the country west of the Mississippi set apart for their permanent residence." This was the Indian removal policy that forced tribes to leave areas east of the Mississippi River. As settlers continued to move west, Native Americans were forced onto smaller and smaller parcels of land as treaties were not honored.

Swampland for Sale—Cheap

The building of Chicago proceeded very slowly. In 1818, there had been just four families living in the marshlands. But there were enough settlers in the rest of Illinois to join the Union as a nonslavery state. Illinois boundaries included the Chicago Portage because it was felt that a harbor and canal there would eventually become a major crossroads between east and west, north and south.

In 1830, John Jacob Astor of the American Fur Company sent an agent to Chicago. But by this time, most natural resources, including the beaver, were scarce, and trade with

As shown in this 1859 cartoon, everyone wanted to buy property in Chicago even though the land was very swampy. In just 50 years, over 300,000 settlers were attracted to the area.

the Indians was a dying business. One trader remarked, "That summer we had little else to do than fight mosquitoes."

That same year, the government sold lots in Chicago for an average of $35 each. Some settlers did not want to buy muddy land that was underwater for half the year. But 17-year-old John Stephen Wright bought two acres of swamp for $25, and two years later, he had made $200,000 in land deals. So did many other speculators. Mud or no mud, once land was for sale, people scrambled to buy it and move to Chicago. In 1833, Chicago was still a muddy trading post with fewer than 100 people. By 1871, the year of the Great Fire, Chicago had a population of 334,000.

The Boom Is On

With land for sale, settlers, innovators, speculators, and desperadoes started to arrive by the thousands. Some had been living on the East Coast, others were new immigrants from Ireland, Germany, and Sweden. Many came to dig out the mud and turn the Chicago Portage into the Illinois and Michigan Canal. On opening day in 1848, 16 ships lined up to pass through the new canal. And the railroads became even more important. Just about every rail line in the United States came through Chicago. Stockyards, grain elevators, lumberyards, tanneries, and fisheries thrived. Wheat, hogs, and cattle from the West were shipped to the East. Clothing and other goods from the East Coast passed through Chicago on their way south and west.

Timberrrr!

Building so close to water was very handy. Logs were floated down from the northern forests as cheap and quick building material. Hammers and saws were the constant sounds of growth. The city had big mud problems, however. When it rained, streets oozed and flooded. Roads might close for weeks as wagons and horses sank deep into the squishy streets. Citizens made jokes and put up signs over potholes: MAN LOST, TEAM UNDERNEATH, STAGE DROPPED THROUGH.

Wood, so abundant that it was sometimes stacked 30 feet high on both sides of the Chicago River, was the solution. Pine blocks were used to pave 55 miles of streets. Wood planks provided 600 miles of raised sidewalks. Twelve wood bridges were built to connect a city cut into three sections by the branches of the river. Wood was used almost everywhere, including houses, streetlamps, wagons, outhouses, sheds, barns, lumberyards, fences, and stoves. It was used in furniture and matchbook factories. Perched above the mud, Chicago became a huge artificial forest, dried out and baking in the sun.

A Convenient River Gets Contaminated

Waste was everywhere, and all of it was dumped into the Chicago River. This allowed a new disease called cholera to threaten the city and spread to the Great Lake tribes. Cholera is caused by bacteria that thrive in unsanitary water and attack the intestines. In 1849, the disease raged through the city. In 1854, it returned, killing about 1,400 people that year and leaving the streets lined with wooden coffins.

At the time, no one understood the link between dirty water and disease. People thought disease was caused by bad odors, or "miasmas," and they continued to use the river as a sewage dump. They did understand the need to fix the drainage, however. In 1856, they tackled the huge job of raising buildings above the swampy ground. It took 1,200 men and 5,000 jack-

Cholera is transmitted to humans by water or food. The bacteria have tails to propel them and to feel for crevices in the small intestine. There, cholera toxins cause cells to release a flood of water and electrolytes. This, in turn, causes diarrhea that washes away competing bacteria and also carries billions of cholera bacteria to new places.

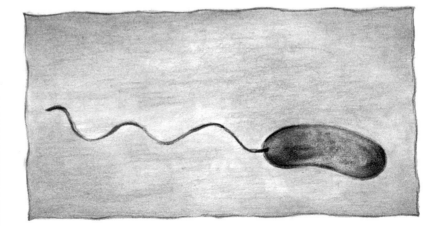

screws just to raise the Tremont House, the largest hotel in the city. Eventually they raised every building in the city limits by 4 to 10 feet. Spaces underneath were to be filled with sand and mud, but sometimes this was neglected. These underground tunnels would provide a flow of oxygen to stoke the Great Fire.

Drinking water from Lake Michigan was still contaminated, and there was another cholera outbreak in 1866. By now, a London physician named John Show had demonstrated that dirty water was a carrier of cholera. Ever inventive, the people of Chicago built a tunnel two miles out into Lake Michigan to pull cleaner water from the middle of the lake. They installed a pump house with four shiny engines to distribute freshwater around the city. The new Chicago Water Works flowed so well that residents no longer had to put up with tiny fish sometimes wriggling out of their kitchen faucets.

A fire needs plenty of fuel, heat, and oxygen to keep burning. Chicago had wooden construction everywhere, with air spaces under sidewalks and buildings to provide extra oxygen. The city had a terrific supply of water, but it came from only one source. There was a professional fire department of 185 men, but it wasn't big enough for the growing population. Windy Chicago, the railroad, meat-packing, lumber, and grain center of the United States, was a fire disaster waiting to happen.

Fire! Fire! Fire!

Then came the drought in 1871. For four months, there was little rain and plenty of hot wind. Leaves and prairie grasses

THE CAUSE OF THE GREAT CHICAGO FIRE OCT. 9 TH 1871.

A WARNING TO ALL WHO USE KEROSENE LAMPS.

Never forget that more lives have been lost, and more comfortable homes burned up by a **Careless Use** of this light than any other ever introduced into common

This 1872 print by W. O. Mull places Mrs. O'Leary in the barn with a cow kicking over a lantern, which resulted in a fire. It was later discovered that Mrs. O'Leary was in bed at the time.

crinkled and crackled. In just one week in October, there were 27 fires. On a Saturday night, October 7, 1871, a huge blaze burned for 16 hours and devoured four blocks. This fire wore out the firemen and left much of their equipment in need of attention.

On Sunday, October 8, shortly after nine o'clock at night, the Great Fire started in the O'Learys' barn. The firemen were already exhausted. Some suffered from inflamed eyes, singed hair, and smoke poisoning. Two fire engines and leather fire hoses were damaged and in need of repair. That day, the *Chicago Tribune* warned, "The absence of rain for three weeks [has] left everything in so dry and inflammable a condition that a spark might set a fire which would sweep from end to end of the city." But the citizens were fire weary. When the Sunday-night fire started and a bell at the courthouse rang out in warning, the editor at the *Tribune*, Horace White, admitted, "I did not deem it worthwhile to get up and look at it, or even to count the strokes of the bell to learn where it was."

A neighbor of Mrs. O'Leary, Daniel "Peg Leg" Sullivan, was the first to see the fire. Mrs. O'Leary and her Irish Catholic immigrant family were already in bed, but a rumor later started that she was milking cows in the barn and the fire ignited when a cow kicked over a kerosene lamp.

A druggist in the neighborhood said he sent in two alarms with the new telegraph system installed at his store. If so, the alarms were never received by the fire watchman at the courthouse. But the watchman did spot smoke in the distance. At first he thought it was embers still smoldering from the Saturday-night fire. Finally he saw rising flames but misjudged the location. He asked his assistant to strike alarm box 342, which directed firemen to a location about one mile from the fire. When he realized his mistake and asked his assistant to strike box 319, the assistant refused because he thought a change would be confusing. Meanwhile, tired firefighters struggled to hitch up tired horses and headed in the wrong direction. The best fire equipment was the last to arrive, and the closest fire hydrant was 11 blocks away. By the time they attacked the fire, six buildings were already burning. As one firefighter said, "From the beginning of that fatal fire, everything went wrong."

The Firestorm

The fire started in a poor part of the city thick with burnable shacks and other wood, kerosene, and hay. The firemen managed to stop the blaze from going west, but "the wind, blowing a hurricane, howling like myriads of evil spirits, drove the flames before it with a force and fierceness which could never be described or imagined," wrote Anna E. Higginson. The flames headed north, jumping over streets and flying high above buildings. They sizzled across sidewalks and fences. Fire Marshal Robert A. Williams sent in alarms for more engines that had to come from miles away.

The blaze got incredibly hot. Joseph E. Chamberlin wrote, "Streams were thrown into the flame, and evaporated almost as soon as they struck. A single fire engine in the blazing forests of Wisconsin would have been as effective." One firefighter used a thick door as a shield, but the door caught fire, his clothes began to smoke, and his leather hat twisted in the terrible heat.

The fire became a firestorm, making its own wind that hurled burning embers and even flaming mattresses through the air. R. Alexander Frear said, "The wind would lift the great body of flame, detach it entirely from the burned buildings, and hurl it with terrific force far ahead." The night grew brighter with showers of glowing embers, a red storm high above the reach of the fire hoses. Flying sparks ignited a fire four blocks away at a mill full of wood furniture. It then burned quickly through a church, a lumber mill, and a

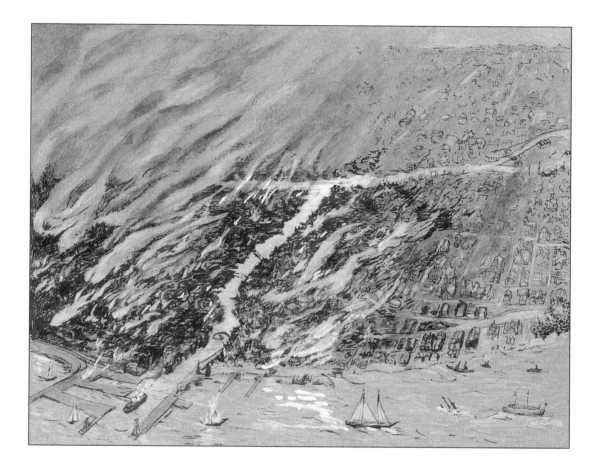

match factory. Desperate people hauled belongings to the street, which just provided more fuel for the fire. The fire marshal was offered $1,000 to save a store. "You might as well offer a million," he responded, "for I could not stop it." In less than three hours, the fire advanced seven blocks northeast.

Everyone hoped it would run out of fuel at the site of the Saturday-night fire, but it did not. A dozen fire engines fighting in three groups were unable to stop it. Firemen had to

Chicago burning in 1871.

pull out as their hoses burned. Fireman Thomas Byrne said, "You couldn't see anything over you but fire. No clouds, no stars. Nothing else but fire." Many citizens helped where they could, but a few began looting and drinking, which added to the chaos.

Fire Jumps the River

The firestorm continued to grow. By 11:30 P.M., it carried the fire clear across the river. The blaze burned quickly through a poor area called Conley's Patch, where many were trapped. Then it headed for the post office, department stores, hotels, opera house, newspapers, and banks. When the fire reached the gasworks, it exploded, leaving much of the city without lights. The watchman in the courthouse was busy ringing the bell as a warning and also stamping out fires that started on the roof. Finally he slid down the banister to escape as the courthouse burned. Prisoners in the basement jail were released just in time. At 2:05 A.M., the massive courthouse bell, which had been ringing for five hours, came crashing down and the ringing stopped.

In this time before telephones, radios, or television, some didn't even know about the event until it was almost too late. Wooden ships and bridges burned, leaving thousands desperate. A "torrent of humanity," along with horses, cows, hogs, dogs, cats, and rats, scattered in the panic. Schools, churches, museums, libraries, and hospitals sizzled in the destruction. Joseph Edgar Chamberlin of the *Chicago Evening*

Post reported, "Collisions happened almost every moment, and when one overloaded wagon broke down, there were enough men on hand to drag it by force."

Twelve-year-old Claire Innes got separated from her family in the confusion.

> A short rough man grabbed at my bundle [but I] would not let go. . . . There was no resisting the crush and we were swept along. I turned around at some point and saw a building burst into flames as if it were built of dry straw. . . . I felt as a leaf . . . in a great rushing river.

Claire saved herself in an alley. "I cannot say I actually decided to hide behind the bricks," but she did, and she was not harmed as an entire block burned around her. Later she went back to her old neighborhood, searching for her family. "Everything was gone," she said. "Where our house had been was nothing but a pile of brick and ash and nothing else." Eventually she saw her father pacing at a burned house down the street and realized that she "had been waiting in front of the wrong house all along."

Some Chicago structures were supposed to be fireproof. The Chicago Tribune building, for instance, was constructed with iron and granite. Unfortunately, the roof was wood covered with tar, and it burned like a torch. The entire inside of the building was gutted. The Sherman House, built of marble, was not fireproof either. Intense flames reduced it to powder. Joseph Medill, publisher of the *Chicago Tribune*, wrote that the business district was "an indescribable chaos of broken columns, fallen walls, streets covered with debris, melted metal, charred and blackened trees standing like spectres."

Blasting Away the Fuel

One man, James Hildreth, had an alternative idea to stop the fire. He wanted to blow up buildings in its path so that it would lose its source of fuel. He obtained blasting powder from the fire marshal and then had to learn how to use it. After several false starts, he blew up some buildings. He may have helped to stop the fire from spreading south. But as he moved to other areas, he couldn't get people to help him. "I tried with a great many, maybe twenty or thirty men, to get them to stop and assist in blowing up the buildings, to stop the fire . . . but I could not get them to stop." People were terrified of his blasting powder. After blowing up dozens of buildings, Hildreth gave up.

The Waterworks Sizzles!

Alongside the firefighters, many people had been pouring water onto buildings, trying to save them. But at 3:20 A.M., the fire reached the waterworks. The wooden roof over the pumps burned, timbers fell into the machinery, and by 4:00 A.M. the pumps had stopped. Without them, fire hydrants were worthless, fire hoses sagged, and the people were helpless. After some 26 hours of devouring the West and South districts, the fire jumped the river again to reach the expensive houses of the North District. Many people were caught sleeping and barely had time to escape. Soon they were running out to the prairie or down to Lake Michigan. Some drove carts and horses into the water. One father managed to save his children from the flames by burying them in the sand at Lincoln Park. They were entirely covered, expect for a small air hole that allowed them to breathe.

Finally at 11 o'clock Monday night, rain began. After 31 hours of burning, the fire was low on fuel and cooling off at the edge of Lake Michigan. Still it sizzled and sputtered through the night while homeless people shivered far out on the prairie and in the cold water of Lake Michigan. Some died from exposure to the chill, and forty babies were born out on the prairie on that cold, wet night.

After the Fire

The fire left 100,000 homeless. About 300 people died. Untold animals were lost, and 18,000 houses and businesses were destroyed. The railroads offered free passage to anyone who wanted to leave the smoldering city, and 40,000 left soon after.

Irma Rosenthal Frankenstein wrote that "the water which our hired girls had collected in the wash tubs was the most precious thing in all of Chicago. People from the whole neighborhood clamored for it to be used for drinking."

Walking past a wife taking care of her sick husband in a piano packing case, a man offered to help. "Her greatest

An enterprising merchant set up shop in the ruins of Chicago.

trouble was want of water and when we gave her a jugful, her gratitude knew no bounds."

With the entire water supply cut off, locomotives pumped water from the lake. Then it was hauled in carts and sold at a high price. Once the flow was finally restored, the water was contaminated and made many people sick.

Army tents were set up in parks and on the prairie for over 60,000 crowded and cold survivors. They were hungry and stressed, and disease once again became a problem. More than 2,000 caught smallpox, and 655 died. Smallpox vaccinations were provided.

Rebuilding happened so quickly that there was no time to think and plan. People with money or insurance could rebuild. Poor people could not. By the end of 1871, there were 6,000 new wood shanties, 2,000 solid wood-frame buildings, and 500 new brick or stone houses. Aaron Montgomery Ward decided to take advantage of the rebuilt transportation network and started the first mail-order catalog business in 1872. No steps were taken to prevent fire hazards until yet another blaze in 1874 destroyed 800 buildings. Following this disaster, the insurance companies refused to insure the city any longer. The city was forced to change.

Chicago now attracted great architects, who developed solutions. In 1885 William Le Baron Jenney designed the first skyscraper, the Home Insurance Building, after figuring out how to make a "raft" for the building to sit on mud and how to use steel, the new material of the industrial age, for framing to hold it up. Skyscrapers changed city life, allowing large numbers of people to live and work together in small areas. Since fire hoses could not reach the higher floors of skyscrapers, new standards for water storage tanks, sprinklers, smoke alarms, fire inspections, and materials were implemented to avoid major urban fires.

Cholera and other waterborne diseases continued to plague Chicago, as did smallpox. In 1885, six inches of rain in one day washed much contamination into Lake Michigan. Waterborne diseases like cholera, typhoid fever, and dysentery ravaged the city, and 12 percent of the population died. Five years later, another cholera epidemic lasted for two years and

Although everything burned around them, the O'Leary house and barn were not destroyed by the fire. The structures were finally torn down in 1956, and the site was used to build an academy to train Chicago firefighters.

left Chicago with one of the highest death rates in the world. When new information proved that cholera was caused by bacteria, the city required everyone to "connect dwellings to sewers." In 1900, another canal was dug to reverse the flow of the Chicago River so that waste could no longer contaminate the source of drinking water.

Who's to Blame?

Everyone was looking for someone to blame, and with plenty of prejudice against Irish immigrants, Mrs. O'Leary and her cow became the target. She was described by Michael Ahern, a *Chicago Republican* reporter, as "in her 70s and on public relief," when actually she was in her 40s and hardworking. She and her husband had saved $500 by 1864 to buy land with two cottages and a barn. Although she was in bed when the fire started, rumor became fact as far as many people were concerned, and life became hard for the O'Learys. Many resented that the O'Leary house was spared in the Great Fire.

The *Chicago Tribune* wrote that "there have been not less than nine hundred causes assigned for the Chicago conflagration." Theories about a milk thief, rat hunters, fire extinguisher salesmen, and mysterious strangers were discussed. One man thought the fire was caused by a comet because two other fires started at the same time. The first, in Peshtigo, Wisconsin, killed around 1,200 people but wasn't nearly as famous because it occurred in a remote logging area. The second blaze, the Port Huron Fire, burned through three cities in Michigan.

Twenty-two years after Chicago's Great Fire, the city was rebuilt enough to host 21 million visitors who came for the World's Columbian Exposition. And finally, in 1997, 126 years after the Great Fire, the Chicago City Council passed a resolution to relieve Catherine O'Leary of responsiblity for starting it.

CHAPTER THREE

Johnstown Flood

May 31, 1889

Welcome to Johnstown

In 1889, Johnstown, in southwest Pennsylvania, was a big
steel-producing town. Seven thousand people worked for the
Cambria Iron Company, where great furnaces melted iron
into steel for rails, barbed wire, farm equipment, ships, and
frames for those new "skyscrapers" going up in Chicago.
Smokestacks spewed soot, and trees on the hillside turned
black and stopped producing leaves. The Pennsylvania

Work in a steel mill was hot, hard, and dangerous.

Railroad whistled in on steel tracks, making deliveries and hauling off steel products.

In the extreme heat of a steel mill, molten metal exploded, floors were slippery, and fires were common. One man who stirred down little spikes of pure iron with a 25-pound spoon said, "I am like some frantic baker in the inferno, kneading a batch of iron bread for the devil's breakfast." It was expensive to let the fires die, so production never stopped. Workers were usually on the job 10 or 12 hours, six days a week, and earned about $10 for the week.

At one point, the steel industry in Johnstown was the largest in the world and a vital place where local farm boys were trained in the new, quick Bessemer process to produce cheap steel. But an influential industrialist named Andrew Carnegie then hired away the best Cambria Iron workers and set up a competing steel mill nearby in 1875. By 1876, production at Carnegie's mill had exceeded that of the Cambria Iron Company.

By the standards of the day, the Cambria Iron Works treated its workers fairly well. One plant, for instance, scheduled an eight-hour day, something desired by factory, mill, and rail workers around the country. Andrew Carnegie had tried an eight-hour workday but abandoned it as profits decreased. The Cambria Iron Works also maintained a hospital where injured employees could receive free treatment.

But most workers at Cambria still rented cheap pine-board company tenement houses situated along the two rivers that flowed through town. Labor unions were not tolerated, and rules stated that anyone who wanted to "control wages or stop the works" could be fired.

Afloat on a Red Tin Roof

On May 31, 1889, the people of Johnstown faced bigger problems than long hours and dangerous work. That day, both rivers rose steadily, inch by inch, through the streets of Johnstown, flooding places they had never reached before. Horace Rose, an attorney who lived downtown, shouted to a friend that this was the "first time we ever saw a cow drink Stony

Creek river water on Main Street." The 7:00 A.M. shift at Cambria mills was sent home and schools closed. The barbed wire plant shut down at 10:00 as the two rivers continued to creep up at the alarming rate of more than a foot an hour.

Sixteen-year-old Victor Heiser sloshed through two feet of water to untie the horses in the family barn. Before he could return to his parents in the house, Victor said his "ears were stunned by the most terrifying noise I had ever heard." He rushed back to the barn and climbed up, up, until he was perched on the red tin roof. Soon he saw

> a huge wall advancing with incredible rapidity down the diagonal street. It was not recognizable as water; it was a dark mass in which seethed houses, freight cars, trees, and animals. As this wall struck Washington Street broadside, my boyhood home was crushed like an eggshell before my eyes, and I saw it disappear.

In a split second, Victor glanced at his watch—4:20 precisely. The next instant, the barn was "ripped from its foundations and started to roll, like a barrel." Victor managed to teeter and stumble on the floating roof until it smashed into the house of a neighbor. In a flash he leaped to the roof of that house. It caved in, so he reached again until he was dangling from the eaves of yet another floating house. His cold fingers clung to the soggy wood until he could hold on no longer. He dropped through the air and somehow managed to plop back onto the red tin roof of his barn.

The flood surged all around, "crushing, crumbling, and splintering everything before it." Victor jumped trees and girders just to remain afloat. Then a railroad freight car loomed over his head. At the last moment, the red tin roof "shot out from beneath the freight car like a bullet from a gun," and he was safe once again. All around, Victor saw people bobbing, floating, struggling, but there was nothing he could do to help.

The great pile of floating debris struck the arches of the stone bridge on the far side of Johnstown and created a dam. In the backwash, the giant wave swept up into another valley and picked up more houses, people, trees, and animals. But the flood slowed a bit, and finally Victor was able to hop to a brick building and join others stranded on the roof.

Six people were in this house when it was skewered by a tree and toppled by a wave. All managed to survive.

Victor took another second to pull out his watch. "It was not yet four-thirty," he said. "Three thousand human beings had been wiped out in less than ten minutes."

The South Fork Fishing and Hunting Club

Where did this great flood come from? In the mountains, 14 miles upriver and 450 feet above Johnstown, a group of wealthy industrialists from Pittsburgh bought, in 1879, an old, neglected dirt dam surrounding a small lake about 10 feet deep. The dam had been built by the state for a canal system, but railroads were replacing canals, and the property was sold to the Pennsylvania Railroad in 1857. The railroad ignored it for years, and then sold it to Congressman John Reilly in 1875. It was the group from Pittsburgh that saw potential—trees, loons, bears, deer, and several ice-cold streams perfect for trout fishing. The lake was 40 feet deep when they bought it, because pipes used to drain the water had been removed by Reilly. Instead of replacing the pipes, they built up the lake until it was 65 feet deep and three miles across. Secretive and exclusive, the South Fork Fishing and Hunting Club was born.

The private club paid plenty of attention to their 47-room clubhouse, huge "cabins," stables, and docks. They brought in sailboats, canoes, and fine fishing gear and stocked the lake with expensive fish. But they paid scant attention to the 900-foot dam that backed up their lake. Like others before them, they never consulted an engineer to make repairs. At one point, hay, branches, rocks, and even loads of horse manure were used for repairs, rather than proper materials required to maintain a dirt dam. The club also scraped off the top level of the dam by several feet to make a two-way carriage road for the comings and goings of members. They installed fish screens, which slowed the flow of water, to keep the fish from escaping. And they never bothered to fix the place where the dike sagged in the middle. Such scrimping and changes left the dam primed for failure.

When first hearing of this business venture, the Cambria Iron Works sent John Fulton, an engineer, out to inspect the dam. He noticed the "want of a discharge pipe" and "unsubstantial method of repair, leaving a large leak," and predicted a break. "Should this break be made during a season of flood, it is evident that considerable damage would occur in the valley." But the man in charge of the dam, B. F. Ruff, was not impressed. He responded that "you and your people are in no danger from our enterprise." The overflow pipes were never replaced.

Neither of these men lived to see the week of torrential rain when the lake rose six inches every hour and became clogged with debris. The townspeople who lived below knew little about the private club and were not allowed to visit. A lake with sailboats in the mountains seemed like a fantasy to them. The dam had failed in the past, but little damage was done. Victor Heiser wrote his neighbors that "that dam will give way, but it won't ever happen to us."

From Rags to Riches

Andrew Carnegie was a member of the club. When he was twelve, he had come to the United States as a poor immigrant from Scotland. His father was a weaver of fine linen but couldn't make a living after a steam-powered textile mill came to town and turned out material much faster than he could by hand. A seven-week voyage brought Carnegie's family to Slabtown, a rough neighborhood across the river from Pittsburgh. Andrew went to work with his father in a textile mill but didn't stay long. He moved on to telegraph, railroad, and other jobs. He invested in railcars and steel mills and eventually became the richest man in the world. He was an immigrant living the American dream.

Two of Carnegie's friends from Slabtown were also members of the club. Henry Phipps, Jr., was a longtime business partner, and Robert Pitcairn ran the Pittsburgh Division of the Pennsylvania Railroad. Other friends with a membership included Andrew Mellon, a banker, and Henry Clay Frick, the head of Carnegie's steel business. Each of the 61 members had spectacular fortunes and lots of influence. A new phrase, "robber baron," came into use in the 1880s; many who worked for these men felt that the men's fortunes were made at the risk and expense of overworked and underpaid employees.

Six members of the private club were at the lake on the day of the flood. When the dam broke, they rode safely out of the mountains on horseback. Andrew Carnegie was attending the World's Fair in Paris and then traveled to his castle in

Scotland. The people of Johnstown did not know he was a member of the secretive club until a year later when the membership list was revealed.

Hear That Train a-Whistlin'

On May 31, John Parke, a newly hired resident engineer, was at the resort, in charge of a crew installing new indoor plumbing. He slept in the clubhouse and woke early in the hammering rain. When he checked outside the ground was soggy. Trees dripped water. Even the air seemed saturated with water. But most alarming was that the lake, he noticed, had risen two feet during the night.

He rode a horse out across the dam. The crew of diggers was piling dirt on top of the dam in an effort to raise it. Others were trying to cut a spillway to drain the rising water, but the area was too rocky.

Stumps, logs, and underbrush had clogged the fish screens. Removal of the big iron screens was urged, but the fish would have been lost so the man in charge said he wouldn't do it. "And then when he said he would do it, it was too late. The screens wouldn't budge." By 11:00 in the morning, it was apparent that all efforts to deal with the surging lake level were failing. The water kept rising and started to wash away the piles of dirt recently added to raise the dam.

The people in the valley below needed to be warned. But how? The telephone had not yet been set up for the summer. John Parke rode his horse to South Fork, but no one took him seriously, including Emma Ehrenfeld, the telegraph operator. Most telegraph lines were down so Emma couldn't send a direct message to Johnstown anyway. But she did tap out a message to the Mineral Point operator, who tapped back that they should take this seriously. A railroad trackman walking by was given a folded message to deliver down the line. Eventually messages reached East Conemaugh, Johnstown, and Pittsburgh.

Meanwhile, the increased flow of water at the dam swelled to a critical point. At about 12:30, Dan Siebert was sent up on horseback to check and returned to report a "glassy sheet of water, fifty to sixty feet wide" pouring over the top. The rain-drenched crowd that had gathered to watch the overflow shuddered as the dam itself began to break. At 3:10 P.M., there was a "roaring like a mighty battle," according to one eyewitness. When the dam failed, the lake seemed to leap into the valley like a living thing. Some estimated it took 35 to 45 minutes for the lake to empty. However long it took, civil engineers later indicated that the bursting of the South Fork dam was like "turning Niagara Falls into the valley for 36 minutes." The flood swept through several small towns, picking up every bush, tree, blade of grass, body, boulder, and building in its path. It took out the Pennsylvania Railroad viaduct and swept through Woodvale, a company town maintained by the Cambria Iron Works. In a few seconds, the population of 1,000, their woolen mill, two schoolhouses, and all other buildings were reduced to nothing.

The pulsating mass continued down the valley at 40 miles per hour, looking like a large hill rolling over and over. As it

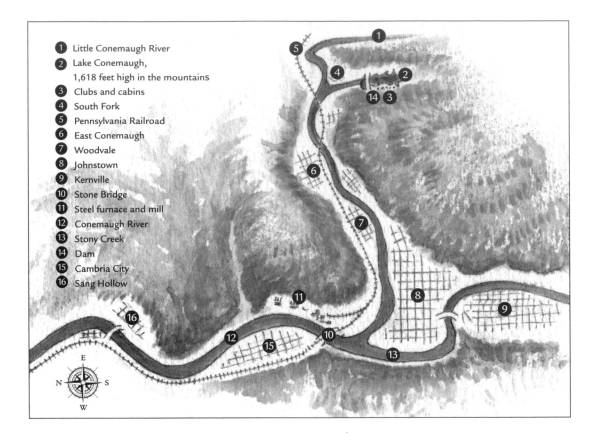

1. Little Conemaugh River
2. Lake Conemaugh,
   1,618 feet high in the mountains
3. Clubs and cabins
4. South Fork
5. Pennsylvania Railroad
6. East Conemaugh
7. Woodvale
8. Johnstown
9. Kernville
10. Stone Bridge
11. Steel furnace and mill
12. Conemaugh River
13. Stony Creek
14. Dam
15. Cambria City
16. Sang Hollow

When the dam broke, the great flood swept away towns in the valley, flooded Johnstown, and backed up into Kernville. Debris piled up at the Stone Bridge and washed on down the river. In Cambria City, two-thirds of the houses were also washed away. Victor Heiser floated from Johnstown to Kernville and spent the first night after the flood in a Kernville attic.

sped along, it collected more bridges, mangled houses, railcars, miles of barbed wire, and acres of trees and dead animals. John Hess, a train engineer, heard the flood coming and put on steam in a race to stay ahead of it. He tied down his whistle and let it blow for five minutes straight. Usually engineers "whistled" their own special tunes as they passed. But a locomotive whistle blowing steadily was a warning. Most who heard "that train a-whistlin'"

knew exactly what it meant and headed for the hills. Along the way, the surge swallowed up 18 locomotives and everything else at the railroad roundhouse.

Victor didn't hear the whistle. It was 4:20 P.M. And what he saw coming at him was so full of debris that he didn't even recognize it as water.

The Cambria iron mills were destroyed by the flood but quickly rebuilt.

The Wreckage

As the flood gushed through Johnstown, it wiped out the new hospital, the library, hotel, roller skating rink, schools, churches, opera house, and saloons. But the Stone Bridge built over the junction of the two rivers did not collapse. Somehow, it held up to the power of 20 million tons of water smashing into it carrying the debris of six towns. The wreckage swirled and whirled, backed up and returned. As water seeped through, a pile of debris 40 feet high was left behind, stacked against the bridge. Some people were able to escape the whirlpool, but many ended up trapped in this crisscrossed tangle. Later a fire started from the fuel tank of an overturned freight train, and flames burned through the night.

Victor spent the night in the attic of the house with 19 others pulled from the flood. As they huddled together in the dampness, he heard damaged houses around them "melt like a lump of sugar and vanish." Every "whoo-oosh . . . meant that another building had sunk."

Dawn brought some relief. The rain stopped, and Victor could see the safety of the higher hills about a half mile away. With others, he rafted and waded through a "mat of debris, broken here and there by patches of dirty water" until he reached solid ground again.

Soon he was helping to rescue people imprisoned in the burning pile of debris at the Stone Bridge. The rescuers lacked axes and shovels. "We could not save them all," Victor said. More than eighty people burned in the bridge fire.

After the Flood

Friends offered Victor a place to live and then he spent weeks looking for his parents: "Everyone I met was on the same sad

errand—looking for parents, children, relatives, or friends."
Many had only wet clothes, no food, and no place to live. Some
died of exposure and injuries before the 10 miles of destroyed
rail lines could be repaired and then tents and supplies brought
in. Great piles of dishes, shingles, chairs, locomotives, and

Debris stacked up 40 feet high at the Stone Bridge. Some people were trapped in the devastation and could not be rescued when the pile started to burn. Crews used railcars to clear the area.

toys were everywhere. Some floated in muddy pools of yellow water. Other debris and bodies were swept downriver past Pittsburgh, where thousands gathered to watch the remains of Johnstown float by.

One man was delighted to locate his young daughter, Gertrude, who had hidden in a cupboard as the water rose, then ended up whirling around on a muddy mattress. Finally a man was able to toss her to safety. Her dad almost didn't recognize her with her blond hair tangled and matted with mud.

Victor found his mother's body, but his father was never identified. He did make another discovery. "By a freak of chance, a chest which had stood in the upper hall of our house was found practically intact on one of the piles of wreckage. In it were my father's Civil War uniform with a large old penny in one pocket, a miscellaneous collection of flat silver, and my mother's Bible." Everything else belonging to his parents had been swept away in the flood. Without any ties to the town, Victor left and became a doctor specializing in treatable diseases in poor countries. He eventually visited 45 countries, saved millions of lives, and wrote a best-selling book, *An American Doctor's Odyssey: Adventures in 45 Countries*, on his experiences.

One hundred and twenty-eight children were orphaned. Ninety-nine entire families went missing. Seventy-eight husbands lost their wives; 123 wives lost their husbands.

On Monday, June 10, the first case of typhoid fever was

reported. Several hundred got sick and 40 died, but doctors worked very hard to stop the waterborne disease quickly.

Ten thousand men were hired to clean up the wreckage. Reporters and photographers showed up by the hundreds. Clara Barton arrived with her growing organization, the American Red Cross, and stayed for five months to provide food and shelter. The reporters wrote much about her and added to her fame. Survivors were interviewed by swarms of reporters from newspapers and publishers, and unusual stories were collected. Twelve books were published about the flood in six months, and many songs, plays, and shows were

For days, people downriver from the flood watched 250 million feet of logs and tons of other debris float by.

produced around the country. So many sightseers came to Johnstown that the railroad stopped selling tickets to those without official business.

The front page of the *New York Times* carried news of the "Nation's Greatest Calamity" for five days after the event. Boston ran front-page stories for 15 days. So many people heard about it that relief came pouring in from around the world. In Paris, Buffalo Bill Cody staged a fund-raising production of his Wild West Show that was attended by the Prince of Wales. A carload of potatoes arrived from Walla Walla, Washington. Schoolchildren sent in nickels and dimes. Prisoners from a penitentiary baked 1,000 loaves of bread. A New York butcher sent 150 pounds of bologna. Eventually almost four million dollars were collected, and this does not include everything that rolled in by train.

The Carnegie mill had been negotiating with workers about their jobs but the talks stopped when the superintendent, Captain Bill Jones, took 300 workers at his own expense to aid in the rescue efforts. The steel company donated $10,000 to the relief fund. The South Fork Fishing and Hunting Club donated $3,000 and 1,000 blankets. Thirty members did not contribute anything.

Only one man from the club, S. S. Marvin, who was in the baking business, went to Johnstown in person to help. One large house at the lake sheltered thirteen families for a while, but most from Johnstown didn't want to live so far up in the mountains.

Gradually, new houses and shops went up all over town

and people returned. The Cambria Works started up again in mid-July. Carnegie and his partner Henry Frick tried to get their employees back to work, but the men wouldn't agree to their terms and went on strike. A three-year agreement was reached and then workers went on strike again at the Homestead Mill. Pinkerton's Detective Agency, a private police force, was called in by Henry Frick, resulting in a violent encounter that became as well known as the Johnstown flood.

Who Was to Blame?

The state of Pennsylvania had built the dam, which was completed in 1852. They did it properly, carefully waterproofing layers of clay, but then the Pennsylvania Railroad let it sit unattended for years. The man in charge of an early renovation was dead. The South Fork Fishing and Hunting Club shaved off the top few feet and failed to replace the discharge pipes. No one consulted an engineer for advice on proper repairs. It was difficult to determine where to place the blame.

Dozens of lawsuits were filed against the club and its members and the railroad. A mother and her eight children sued the club for $50,000 for the loss of her husband. Another woman sued for the loss of her father, mother, and brother. Other suits were filed, and many dragged on for years, often moving from county to county as the club looked for friendly juries. "Not a nickel was ever collected through damage suits from the South Fork Fishing and Hunting Club or from any of its members," reported historian David McCullough. A Philadelphia company sued the railroad for the loss of 10 barrels of whiskey. This became the only lawsuit ever won against the railroad because a train conductor admitted that he had looked "the other way when the whiskey was taken."

The Great Giveaway

In May 1889, just before the flood, Andrew Carnegie published a magazine article called "Wealth." He wrote that "the man who dies rich dies disgraced." He felt that, unfair though it may be, the rich and the poor would always exist. So a rich man must divide his life into two parts: First, he should build up a fortune; then he should give it away. "I'm not going to grow old piling up, but in distributing."

At the time of the flood, Carnegie was busy building his fortune. His organization did donate $10,000 to the Johnstown fund and he also built a new library to replace the one that had been lost. But his contribution to the victims of the flood was small considering that he had been the richest man in the world and eventually gave away $324,657,399, which was most of his wealth.

Once he really got started, Carnegie received 400 or 500 letters daily from people making requests. The makers of Mother Seigel's Syrup sponsored a contest: "How Mr. Carnegie Should Get Rid of His Wealth." Thousands of people responded, some requesting money for themselves.

Carnegie gave four million dollars to support employees

of Carnegie Steel Company injured on the job and to the families of those who were killed on the job. He provided old-age pensions for former workers, poorly paid professors, and such famous people as Rudyard Kipling and Booker T. Washington. He

Andrew Carnegie made a fortune in the steel business and eventually gave most of it away, including millions to create libraries around the country.

contributed to marine biology studies, international peace, and many other causes and projects.

His biggest contribution established 2,507 free public libraries, about 1,680 in the United States and the rest in other countries. "I believe," he wrote, "that it outranks any other one thing that a community can do to benefit its people. It is the never failing spring in the desert."

More Floods, Less Steel, and the Money Trail

Johnstown, Pennsylvania, the city between two rivers, was slowly rebuilt. Floods continued to be a problem, including devastating floods in 1936 and 1977. The dam in the mountains was never rebuilt, the lake never refilled, and the club members never returned to their private resort.

Big blast furnaces are a thing of the past in the United States, including Johnstown. Most steel today is produced in "mini" mills that recycle scrap iron.

In 2003, the average worker's wages rose 0.6 percent. In the same period, bosses—chief executive officers and the like—received a 16 percent salary increase and a 20 percent hike in bonus pay. Similar to the 1800s, rich bosses and poor workers still exist.

Bill Gates, founder of Microsoft and one of the richest men in the world, has followed the example of Andrew Carnegie and is giving away much of his wealth. Already the Gates Foundation has helped to save at least 700,000 lives in poor countries by providing vaccinations and other health care.

CHAPTER FOUR

San Francisco Shaking

April 18, 1906

Gold! Gold! Gold! Gold!
Bright and yellow, hard and cold,
Molten, graven, hammered, and rolled,
Heavy to get and light to hold.

—from "Gold!" by Thomas Hood

Gold Fever!

In 1847, only a few hundred settlers lived around the vast wetlands, sand dunes, and oak trees of San Francisco Bay.

Native Americans collected acorns and pounded them into flour. They taught early settlers how to use the acorns in their cooking.

Elk, acorns, berries, salmon, shellfish, marsh grasses, and shorebirds were plentiful, and dozens of Native American tribes depended on them for survival.

In 1848, James W. Marshall, a carpenter, found gold in the foothills of the nearby Sierra Mountains. The tiny settlement of San Francisco exploded into a booming "gold rush" city just as California joined the United States at the end of the Mexican War. Californios, the local Spanish-speaking ranchers, headed for the gold fields.

Native Americans went too. Walter Colton wrote about the spreading excitement when "the blacksmith dropped his hammer, the carpenter his plane, the mason his trowel, the farmer his sickle, the baker his loaf, and the tapster his bottle. All were off for the mines."

As word spread, people showed up from all over the world. Factory workers, farmers, and adventurers looking for a better life jammed the overland trails to the West as soon as the snow melted in 1849. Called the forty-niners, they experienced many hardships, including a raging cholera epidemic during the journey through Missouri. Some impatient gold seekers preferred to crowd onto ships that sailed around the tip of South America or took a shorter route, which required a dangerous overland trek, through Panama. Here they risked not only cholera, but also malaria and other tropical diseases. Any of the journeys could take months, and some forty-niners died of scurvy, a disease caused by vitamin C deficiency, because they were without an adequate supply of fruits and vegetables. As gold seekers demanded faster travel, clipper ships were developed for speed. In 1851, the *Flying Cloud* raced from New York around South America to San Francisco in a record-setting 89 days.

When stories of gold reached China, thousands of people wanting to flee war and poverty sailed across the Pacific to Jiujinshan, the "Old Gold Mountain." In San Francisco, some settled together in several city blocks near the waterfront, creating the first place in the world known as Chinatown. With their different language and culture, they became targets for suspicion, fear, and prejudice.

The San Francisco harbor eventually filled with over 600 abandoned ships when navy, whaling, and fishing crews deserted for the gold fields. As a hundred thousand gold seekers were lured to the area, the need for food, lumber, and mining supplies became desperate. Flimsy buildings were thrown together, and the city burned down six times in two years. Periodic earthquakes caused damage too. All rubble was dumped into the bay, along with rotting ships. Vessels in better shape were run ashore and remodeled as buildings. Gold worth over two billion dollars was eventually found, but riches also came to those who sold food, lumber, and services at high

Miners looking for every possible way to extract gold made destructive changes to the hills.

prices. Levi Straus, for instance, arrived from New York with blue canvas. He made inexpensive, durable clothes for the miners and was able to start a thriving business selling blue jeans.

The rush for gold was wild and lawless. What with fighting, poor food, and little medicine, one in five miners died. Many never found gold. Disappointed, they drifted back to San Francisco, and the city ended up with far too many people for the jobs available. Some blamed the Chinese for the glutted labor market, and several unsuccessful schemes were hatched over the years to send them home.

As the search for gold became overcrowded and desperate, the beautiful hills, valleys, and bay took a beating. The stream-beds were drained and sifted, and new dams blocked the natural flow of water, which was now polluted. Trees were logged, rocks were blasted into pieces, and long mining tunnels were burrowed into eroding hillsides. But the biggest loss was to the Native Americans, who suffered from new diseases, and were kidnapped, enslaved, and murdered. Their numbers decreased from 150,000 to 30,000 in the few years of a gold rush that transformed the West.

A Shaky History

When the gold was gone, San Francisco continued to grow as it developed a reputation for sunshine and good farmland. With the completion of the transcontinental railroad in 1869, immigrants could travel from Omaha to San Francisco in just four days, and they came by the thousands. The city grew by filling in marshes and lakes, moving great volumes of sand, and building over this filled land.

Every year, dozens of earthquakes were felt because the city sits over what is called the San Andreas Fault, where two large sections of earth, the Pacific and North American plates, bump into each other. At that time people didn't know what caused earthquakes, but history had shown them that mud and filled land were not good places to build. A severe earthquake in 1868 demonstrated that structures built in squishy places were the ones most likely to quiver and tumble. It also revealed

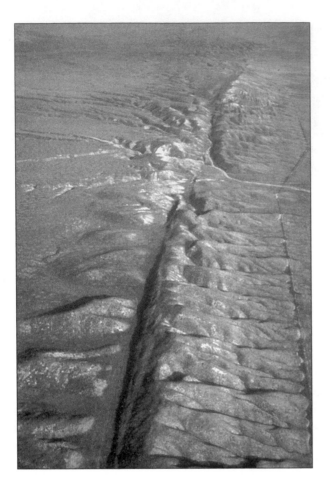

The San Andreas Fault runs 500 miles through California and is one of many pressure points in the earth's crust that cause earthquakes in the San Francisco area.

that brick chimneys failed and fires escaped to rage through wood structures.

Still, in 1906, most of the 400,000 people in San Francisco lived and worked in wood buildings, and everyone had brick fireplaces. Whole sections had been built on filled land over lakes, creeks, seabed, and rubble at a great cost to clean air and water. The bay was a smelly cesspool, where fish and shellfish were dying. The air was choked with coal soot, and streets reeked with the droppings of thousands of horses. But the biggest problem was the earth itself. The plates, constantly grinding and groaning, were about to unleash a catastrophic shudder with enough magnitude to destroy the golden city of the West.

Waking to a Shaking

At 5:12 A.M., Wednesday, April 18, 1906, the bumping plates of earth suddenly made a severe shift. While 300 miles of land tried to settle into a stable position, the shaking sent out waves traveling at almost 6,000 miles per hour and strong enough to be felt in Oregon, Nevada, and southern California. San Francisco, so close to the epicenter, shook severely. Windows broke, ceilings crashed, buildings slumped, and church bells clanged. One man saw the street "dance and rear and roll in waves. . . . Everywhere men were on all fours in the street, like crawling bugs." Another reported a "creaking, grinding, rasping sound," while others were kept "pretty busy for a while dodging bricks."

The first tremor lasted less than a minute. More followed. Cattle stampeded through the city and tumbled into a crack.

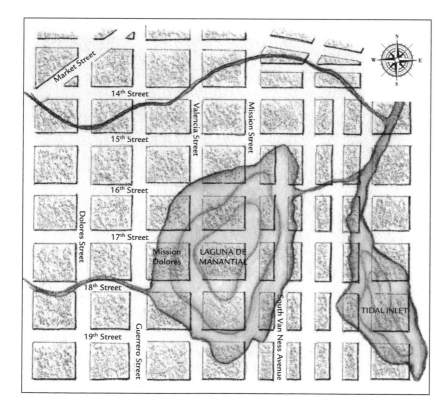

Like the Mission District shown on this map, some areas of San Francisco were built right over filled-in lakes and tidal inlets. In the earthquake, structures in these areas suffered much more damage than those built on solid ground.

Apartments built over mud shook like jelly and toppled. Houses built over creeks lurched and collapsed. Brick buildings tumbled into piles of rubble. Chinatown went down "like a house of cards." The Valencia Hotel, built over a filled marsh, sank into water, and those trapped inside drowned. New buildings at Stanford University crumbled. The "earthquake-proof" City Hall, recently completed after 26 years, revealed its bad design and poor materials as it toppled. At museums, famous paintings, historical documents, and rare bird specimens were buried, but a collapsing library being built with funds from Andrew Carnegie was too new to have any books.

Dennis Sullivan, the San Francisco fire chief, dashed out of bed as his house shook, but bricks from a tumbling smokestack knocked him unconscious. He never recovered. The military took command and sent out 1,500 soldiers with rifles, bayonets, and orders to shoot looters. But as the disaster unfolded, water buckets would have been more useful equipment.

Fifty Fires!

In the violent quake, stoves crashed, and almost every chimney crumbled. Fires started. Wires were severed and gas pipes burst. More fires sprang up. There was the Girard House Fire, the Gas and Electric Fire, and the Chinese Laundry Fire. At 10:30 A.M., a woman cooking breakfast in a broken chimney started the "Ham and Eggs Fire," which eventually became the

largest of about 50 blazes. The fires created their own wind, spread quickly, and joined together. Firefighters, police, and army troops tried to douse them, but the quake had fractured thousands of pipes, and few hydrants had water. When they tried the sewers, they found them "dry or filled with mud." Citizens attempted to snuff out flames with coats and brooms, but the military ordered a quick evacuation, and there was little time to fight. By noon, a wall of fire spread out a mile and a half. Within 12 hours, half the city was crackling.

The military took over most wagons and cars, so people fled

Major pipes bringing water to San Francisco from the mountains were severely damaged in the earthquake.

pushing baby carriages, toy carts, and boxes on roller skates. Steel buildings and houses on solid ground that had survived the quake were now blackened by fire. Eight carloads of opera costumes from New York went up in flames. Millions of dollars' worth of military equipment headed for the Philippines burned. But 46 workers at the post office refused military orders to leave and managed to save the mail by plugging windows with mail sacks soaked in water. Even before the fires were out, they were able to provide service. A botanist from the Academy of Science rescued rare plant samples. Many sick and injured victims were saved by being transported from one place to another just ahead of spreading flames. Workers at the U.S. Mint guarded $200 million in gold coin and bullion stored in the vaults. As all banks were burning, this became the first available money to rebuild the city.

Golden Gate Park and the beaches filled with refugees. Those trying to reach the ferry that would take them across the bay to Oakland or Berkeley walked miles around the fire. They passed areas where no buildings stood in any direction. Jerome B. Clark said, "Nearly all the docks caved in or sheds were knocked down, and all the streets along the water front were a mass of seams, upheavals and depressions, car tracks twisted in all shapes." The Southern Pacific railroad managed to repair its main track out of San Francisco, and thousands crowded into and onto the railcars until "every inch of every piece of rolling stock was occupied by human beings who wanted to flee the burning city." Over the next 96 hours, Southern Pacific provided free train and ferry service that carried away 225,000 refugees. Another chaotic rescue was made along the shoreline. Tugboats, Chinese junks, Navy launches, Italian fishing vessels, and all sorts of private boats hauled 20,000 people away from approaching fire.

Quick Action

By noon of the first day, Mayor Eugene Schmitz set up the Committee of Fifty, made up of leaders in the city willing to help. He sent a message to Oakland across the bay. "Send fire engine, hose, also dynamite immediately." Governor George Pardee requested help from Los Angeles, and by midnight of the first day, their trainload of food, medical supplies, doctors, and nurses arrived. A large hospital train was sent out from Virginia. Congress met the next morning and sent five military relief trains. President Teddy Roosevelt also dispatched West Coast warships and fireboats so that water could be pumped from the bay.

Meanwhile, the fires continued to rage. With the water supply in ruins, blowing buildings "to atoms" seemed the only solution. Inexperienced firefighters tried to dynamite areas to create firebreaks. Jerome Clark, a businessman, said, "They took half a block; that was no use: then they took a whole block, but in spite of them all, the fire kept spreading." The blasting added more tottering walls and flying rubble. A medicine factory was dynamited, and the alcohol inside started a new fire. Eventually three skilled engineers started to blast Van Ness Avenue. Every fire engine in the city was ordered to help, and a few even found hydrants with a weak supply of water. Twenty-two blocks of the wide avenue were destroyed, and the effort was enough to stop the flames in this direction.

The fires burned for three days and destroyed 490 city blocks—28,188 buildings, including 31 schools—and left 225,000 people homeless. One hundred thousand people were camped outside and cooking in the street. Lack of food and water were severe problems. On the first night, a quake-damaged bakery managed to bake 50,000 loaves of bread. The mayor ordered the police to "smash the stores open." As trains and steamers loaded with food and tents rushed in, the situation improved. The post office collected mail from the camps, and anything flat was accepted, no stamps required. William Burke, the postmaster's secretary, reported on the collection: "Bits of cardboard, cuffs, pieces of wrapping paper, bits of newspapers with an address on the margin, pages of books, and sticks of wood all served to let somebody in the outside world know that friends were alive and in need among the ruins."

Pick-up Bricks and the Rat Patrol

Bricks were once again revealed to be a terrible building choice for a shaking city. Thirty-one million of them were piled up on every street and every alley. Everyone was expected to spend some time picking up bricks. New rail tracks were

This group called their temporary home the "House of Mirth" and posted humorous signs referring to an elevator and running water.

laid in parts of the city, and 15,000 loads were needed to haul away debris. Tens of thousands of horses were also used, and many of them were overworked. Three shifts of workers toiled, day and night, to haul off the 15,000 horses that died. The rubble, which included bones and ashes, was dumped into the bay. This became a filled-in wetland where the Marina district was eventually built. In another big earthquake in 1989, this squishy area suffered the most damage.

The campers made use of whatever materials they could

find. Shelters were patched together from bedclothes, rugs, raincoats, bed quilts, and lace curtains. Holes were dug in the streets for latrines, while hundreds of plumbers started to repair water and sewer pipes, a task that would take three years. Meanwhile, a new firm called Odorless Excavators, Inc., used mules and wagons to haul off waste. Smallpox broke out in one camp; thousands of vaccines were given, and the sick were quarantined. Polluted water caused the spread of typhoid, and everyone was ordered to boil water for 30 minutes. With good instructions and adequate medical supplies, these health problems did not become epidemics.

As the city struggled with rebuilding and waste removal, the rat population exploded. Bubonic plague broke out in May 1907. Plague was not new to San Francisco. It had appeared briefly in 1900 when a ship arrived from Hong Kong with a sick stowaway. The disease had been confined to Chinatown and contained with quarantine and the burning of infected houses. Officials spent much time and energy denying to the world that the problem existed.

In 1907, city officials understood more about plague and now knew that the disease was transmitted by fleas on infected rats. Quickly they offered money for dead rats and collected them for testing. They also required concrete flooring, a new rat-resistant material, to be poured in all rat breeding areas. Two million rats were poisoned, 160 people got the plague, and 77 died.

In spite of problems, most people were hopeful. A mother waiting in a long food line with two children said, "I have money if I could get to it and use it. I have property if I could realize on it. I have friends if I could get to them. Meanwhile I am going to cook this piece of bacon on bricks and be happy."

"Fifteen years ago I started with these," said a man showing his hands. "And I guess I'm game to do it over again."

Don't Mention the "E" Word

After April 18, 1906, San Francisco had an image problem. Earthquake? What earthquake? Don't mention that terrible "e" word. For the sake of good public relations, the tourist industry, and East Coast investments, the word was practically erased from history. The Real Estate Board passed a resolution that "the great earthquake" should be replaced by "the great fire." The Southern Pacific started a slick magazine to rebuild the city's image without the "e" word because this mention was "bad for the good repute of the West Coast, and . . . likely to keep away business and capital. Therefore the less said the better." An agent quickly added that the broken water pipes and loss of the water supply should be attributed to the sinking of swampland.

Societies for geologists and engineers urged members not to gather information on the San Andreas Fault and especially not to publish it. Carefully, the past was reimagined and revised until people who had experienced the shaking were thinking the city was destroyed by fire—a careless, preventable event that could befall any city.

There were other reasons for emphasizing fire over the "e"

word. The first 2,000 men who filed insurance claims swore that their properties were uninjured by the earthquake. This was because insurance covered fire damage but not damage from an earthquake. In this disaster, thousands of photos were taken because an inexpensive Kodak camera with roll film had recently turned photography into a popular hobby. These images became very valuable, bought up by the insurance companies to prove earthquake damage, unless they could be destroyed first by those claiming fire damage.

The city reported a death toll of 478. A thorough investigation in the 1980s by Gladys Hansen and Emmet Condon found that the total was 3,000 or more. The Chinese, Japanese, and other minority groups were not included in the lists, nor were people who died of related problems. Officials kept the number low to make the disaster seem less serious.

The "Paper People"

After the fire, the Chinese were sent to separate relief camps, as were the Japanese. Residents in Berkeley, across the bay from San Francisco, put up signs reading NO CHINESE and NO JAPANESE. Thousands crowded into "Chinese-only" relief camps in Oakland.

Within six days, a group called the General Relief Committee composed of five men with longstanding prejudice against the Chinese devised yet another scheme to get rid of them and take control of prime Chinatown property. They wanted the Chinese to move their community to "Oriental City," far away from the waterfront.

The answer was no! Chinese officials and the Empress Dowager, the ruler in China, demanded the rebuilding of Chinatown at the original site, where they owned property and intended to rebuild their consulate.

Many other Californians supported Chinatown too. Eventually it was rebuilt on the same land with new designs inspired by Chinese architecture. The new Chinatown emerged mysterious and unique, has become a prime tourist and business attraction, and supports valuable trade with China.

Many Chinese wanted to come to Chinatown but had been prevented by the Chinese Exclusion Act of 1882, which allowed immigration only for those who already had a relative living in the United States. After the 1906 disaster, all papers needed to prove citizenship were burned. It then became possible for anyone to claim a son, mother, or bride living in the United States. Who could prove otherwise? Those inventing a new family tree were called "paper people." Immigration officials developed hundreds of questions to trip them up. What was the eldest brother's favorite breakfast? Who sat where in the mah-jongg games? Applicants were sometimes locked up for months without visitors while officials checked on their answers. The Chinese Exclusion Act, the first immigration law ever directed at a specific group of people, was finally repealed when China became an ally of the United States in World War II.

Living Along a Fault Line

Today, seven million people live in the Bay area, eight times more than in 1906 when the big earthquake measured 8.3 on the Richter scale. Now an earthquake of this size or larger would cause much more damage, especially if an oil terminal, nuclear facility, or biological research lab was involved. The San Andreas Fault has been moving an inch and a half each year since 1906, to become 17 feet out of kilter. Someday it will reach another critical snapping point. Has the city made enough changes to survive another massive shaking?

After 1906, the city rebuilt its water system to maintain a constant supply. It wrote new codes requiring people to construct buildings to higher safety standards but only enforced these for a short time. Today there are many wood buildings built close together with no fire barriers between them. Since 1972, other new codes have prevented schools, hospitals, power plants, and homes from being built near the fault lines. Scientists test new materials and designs on a "shake table" to see how everything holds up. Architects use this information to create buildings with springy bases made of reinforced and bendable materials. Long bridges across the bay have been strengthened, and most tall buildings are earthquake proof.

Every year about 10,000 earthquakes shake California, and half a million occur around the world. Most are small, but a few are big enough to cause damage. Can the next big one be predicted? Near San Francisco, a thousand earth-

EARTHQUAKE
WARNING
"THIS IS AN UNREINFORCED
MASONRY BUILDING. YOU MAY
NOT BE SAFE INSIDE OR NEAR
UNREINFORCED MASONRY
BUILDINGS DURING AN
EARTHQUAKE."

Today, warning signs are put on many old buildings that have not been improved for earthquake safety.

quake stations have been set up to detect shock waves. A sensor has been installed 10,000 feet deep into the San Andreas Fault, looking for patterns that might signal a rupture. Early-warning studies are also being conducted with birds, snakes, chemical mixes, gases, and satellite radar images. Every day, thousands of microearthquakes, too small to be felt but recorded by sensitive equipment, are being analyzed. Still, scientists don't yet know where or when the next quake will occur.

In 2005, an earthquake in Pakistan claimed 87,000 lives, injured 50,000, and left more than three million homeless.

Millions of other people in cities such as Tehran, Iran, and Istanbul, Turkey, live above major fault lines. If the science of earthquake prediction can be improved, people around the world will benefit.

The New "Gold"

Because it is not yet possible to know when and where the next quake will shake, San Franciscans are taking a closer look at other important things, like water. In their part of the world, water comes from streams in the Sierras that fill with melting snow and glaciers. Everyone pulls water from this flow for toilets and toothbrushing, swimming pools and golf courses, irrigation and manufacturing. Over the last century, people in California, Oregon, and Nevada have been fighting over this water. Today, with millions of new people and with glaciers melting away in a warmer world, the fight is getting much more serious. The supply is valuable but limited, and it is the key to healthy people, salmon, butterflies, insects, birds, shellfish, and everything else. Water is the new gold.

Around the bay, 95 percent of the ecosystem that existed before the gold rush is gone. The water is polluted, and native plants and animals have disappeared. These problems have led residents back to the wetlands, lakes, and creeks that were altered or buried during the gold rush, fires, and earthquakes. The words of John Muir, a conservationist who loved the

Sierras, have helped to inspire them: "Let us do something to make the mountains glad."

Volunteer work parties and munching goats are cleaning out weeds that don't belong. Native California plants like oak trees and purple needlegrass, able to survive 150 years without extra water, are being planted. A natural flow of water is being restored to mudflats so healthy shellfish and shorebirds can thrive once again. And everyone hopes that water will always be in plentiful supply to put out the fires of the next San Francisco shaking.

CHAPTER FIVE

Triangle Shirtwaist Factory Fire

March 25, 1911

O, sing me a song of the Factory Girl,
So merry and glad and free.
The bloom on her cheeks, of health it speaks!
O, a happy creature is she!

—Anonymous

Imagine that you are an immigrant child in the early 1900s, familiar with this popular song. You have come, along with

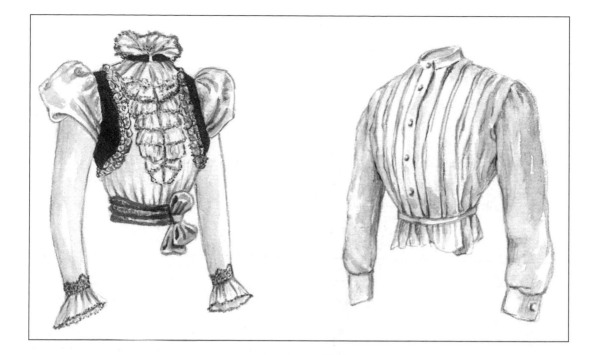

millions of other immigrants, to the United States, hoping to build a comfortable life. Unfortunately, your father dies. Your mother goes to work in a factory, where she sews shirtwaists, the cotton blouses with puffed sleeves that so many women prefer.

At work, men hold all the best positions as supervisors and cutters. Your mother works as a seamstress and earns only half as much. She must rent a sewing machine, the crate that she sits on, and the locker where she hangs her coat. She pays for thread, electricity, and broken needles. The workroom door is kept locked so she can't slip out. At the end of the day, her pocketbook is searched to make sure that she hasn't stolen a wispy thread or swirl of pretty ribbon.

Shirtwaists, worn with long skirts, were popular in the early 1900s until one-piece dresses became the rage. These blouses came in plain, flouncy, and puffy designs.

Young workers in weaving mills climbed up on the spinning frames to mend broken threads and replace bobbins. Many children worked in bare feet in an effort to keep from slipping, which made things worse when accidents occurred.

She works long hours but can't make enough money for the family to survive, so you are working there too. You wear no shoes because bare feet make it easier to climb on the machinery to replace empty spools of thread. This is your job: spooler. Your brother works as a sweeper. The factory is on the top floors of a ten-story building where workers must endure stifling hot summers and icy cold winters.

This garment factory is called a sweatshop. Dust is everywhere, flying off cut threads, fabric, and spinning spools like "a thousand dandelions gone to seed and blown by the wind." Some 240 sewing stations are squeezed

around eight long tables. Everyone coughs in the stuffy room, and many workers have bronchitis. A dangerous lung infection called tuberculosis is also passed around, and several children have mangled feet or hands from accidents around the machinery. You have never been to school and can't read or write, not even your name. Children under 14 are not supposed to work here, but the supervisor hides you in a fabric bin if there is an inspection. You are eight years old,

Crowded tables, dusty air, dangling patterns, and piles of scraps create hazardous working conditions in sweatshops.

work long hours, and are paid just a dollar fifty for a seven-day week. Your mother manages to collect six dollars. Your family shares a small tenement apartment with six other people, and often when you walk home from work, it is much later than you think. Your tricky boss sometimes sets the clock back and no one owns a watch. With this tactic, none of you realize that you have worked an extra hour without pay.

From Slavery to Slave Wages

After the Civil War, the United States moved into the industrial age with many growing problems. For one thing, without slavery, how could the demand for cheap workers be met? Many factories would not hire freed slaves. Instead, they turned to the immigrants who were flooding into the country desperate for jobs. These adults and children were quickly employed as cheap labor in every part of the country. A four-year-old might spend long hours shucking oysters. A three-year-old might sit all day with her family gluing paper flowers or making cigars. A ten-year-old could be snapping beans at a cannery. And small boys spent their days underground hauling lumps of coal.

Immigrant workers were often tricked and bullied. Factory agents were sent out to lure children from farms, promising easy jobs and high wages. The agents were paid a dollar for each child and more if they brought them from such a distance that they could not easily return home.

Workers began to protest but found that the government, police, bosses, and judges did not support their efforts to improve working conditions. Protesters were often beaten, fined, and sent to jail. Some were blacklisted, as employers circulated lists of people in unions who were not to be hired.

The Uprising of the 20,000

On September 27, 1909, two male leaders among the workers at the Triangle Shirtwaist Factory in New York City asked for more money for themselves and the girls in their group. The factory occupied the top three floors of the 10-story Asch Building at Washington Place and Greene Street. The boss ordered them "to get back to the machines." Five minutes later, two thugs came over, "broke the threads of the cotton spools," and told the men to leave the building. When Jake Klein refused, he was grabbed by the neck, dragged to the door, and slapped. With torn shirt and broken glasses, he called out, "People . . . workers . . . look what they are doing to us . . . get up from your machines." Work stopped as hundreds of women and girls followed Jake to the street and later to the office of the International Ladies' Garment Workers' Union, called the ILGWU.

The girls who dared to leave the building were mostly young Jewish and Italian immigrants. Men had gone out on strike in steel, railroad, and mining industries, but a walkout by women and girls was unheard of. This bold action grabbed attention throughout the city. In spite of the risks, young female

At a 1909 labor parade in New York City, girls carried banners written in both English and Yiddish urging the end of child slavery.

workers were protesting, asking for safer work areas, unlocked doors, fire escapes, shorter workweeks, and better wages.

The ILGWU had only 400 members at the time and little money to help, but they called a general strike of all shops to be held on November 22. It became known as the "Uprising of the 20,000" as workers from shirtwaist shops all over New York City joined them. The work stoppage lasted 14 weeks. Young girls joined picket lines outside the factories. Often they were beaten and taken to jail in groups. By Christmas, 723 of them had been arrested and fined; some were sent to Blackwell's Island prison.

But the protesters had allies. Middle- and upper-class women had joined with workers in another union called the Women's Trade Union League (WTUL). Some were suffragists, people who thought women should have the right to vote as men did—something that was not yet legal. These reformers marched with shirtwaist makers on the picket lines. They used the value of their mansions to provide bail money so those arrested could be released from jail. They testified for the protesting workers when possible and provided advice on the best way to run a picket line: no yelling, no threats, no touching, and, please, write down the number of the police officer who arrests you. One wealthy woman, Mary Dreier, a WTUL leader, was also arrested, but the judge let her go quickly. This angered many people, who saw it as another example of how unfairly the workers were being treated.

The strike was very effective for the ILGWU. The union signed contracts with 354 shirtwaist firms, who agreed to improve working conditions by establishing a 52-hour workweek, providing better wages, no longer charging for supplies, and making other improvements.

But the strike that began at the Triangle Shirtwaist Factory was lost at the Triangle Shirtwaist Factory. There, the owners replaced striking workers with new workers, called strikebreakers or scabs. They continued to pay the old wages. They continued to lock the heavy steel door to keep workers from walking out in protest, leaving early, or taking a bathroom break. The wobbly fire escape was not replaced. And workers were still crowded into small spaces with piles of flammable fabric, sewing oil, thread, and dust.

The Triangle Shirtwaist Factory was a fire hazard waiting for ignition. And on March 25, 1911, barely a year after the strike had ended, a great blaze raced through its work areas. The same policemen who had clubbed and arrested girls on picket lines now watched in horror as they jumped from high windows to escape the flames. Martha Bensley Bruère said they had the gruesome task of keeping "the thousands in Washington Square from trampling upon their dead bodies, sent for ambulances to carry them away and lifted them one by one into the receiving coffins."

Fire in the Sweatshop!

The fire started in a rag bin on the eighth floor. To Dominick Cardiane on the street it sounded "like a big puff." As smoke and sizzle filled the room, cutters threw pails of water on the flames. Others hauled in a fire hose, but it was rotten. Quickly the fire spread to fabric scraps and the wood floor. The air filled with smoke and flaming tissue-paper patterns. A call was made to warn the 270 workers on the ninth floor. Nobody answered. Another alarm to the top floor, where all the executives were, went through, and the fire department was notified.

It was payday, Saturday afternoon. Most of the men had already received their wages and left the building. But other employees, mostly young women, were milling around, wait-ing to be paid. As the flames spread, they were trapped in crowded rows. Some tried to climb over the sewing machines. As fire blocked one narrow stairway, many swarmed to the second stairway. "The door was locked," said one survivor, "and immediately there was a great jam of girls before it." Others pressed elevator buttons in panic. Someone remembered a fire escape outside and broke a shuttered window to reach it.

Firemen arrived within minutes, but by then all three floors were ablaze. Their ladder only reached to the sixth floor. They could see workers gathering on window ledges, screaming for help.

When the executives on the 10th floor received the warning, they called for the elevators. The men who operated the elevator cars went right past the eighth floor and up to the top to pick up passengers. Then they stopped at eight. Thirty people crowded into cars meant to hold half that many. "There wasn't enough room for a pin in that elevator," said a survivor. After several trips, the elevators could no longer operate in the heat and flames. When Joseph Zito's elevator refused to move up, he heard thumps on his roof. "A body struck the top of the elevator and bent the iron," he said. Some lucky girls managed to grab the elevator cable and slide down 90 feet, but others died in the elevator shaft.

Those left on the 10th floor were making their way to the roof. This included owner Max Blanck and his two small daughters, who had been visiting. Students and workers from New York University next door extended ladders and helped them to escape. Except for one jumper, all 70 people on the 10th floor were saved.

The first people on the fire escape made it to the sixth floor. Then they went back inside the building and found themselves trapped behind another locked door. Sixteen-year-old Abe Gordon, a belt boy, said, "I still had one foot on the fire escape when I heard a loud noise and looked back up. The people were falling all around me." A fireman eventually chopped through the door, but fewer than 20 were able to use the fire escape before it collapsed. Back on the ninth floor, Rose Cohen saw this scene: "Girls were lying on the floor fainted. People were stepping over them. Some were running with their hair burning." Dozens were found trapped in the dressing room, where they had burned to death.

Thousands of spectators gathered outside to watch. In horror, they saw girls standing at windows, flames licking at

This fire escape was blocked by a locked window and ended at the second floor, 20 feet off the ground. It bent and collapsed under the weight of the workers who had finally managed to reach it.

their skirts, their hair smoldering. From 80 feet up, they tied rags around their eyes, held hands, and jumped in groups of as many as five. Firemen opened life nets but three bodies struck the first net at the same time and carried the nets to the sidewalk. "The force was so great it took the men off their feet. . . . The men's hands were bleeding, the nets were torn, and some caught fire. What good were life nets?" asked Battalion Chief Edward J. Worth.

The employees sewing shirtwaists on the ninth floor had their escape blocked by back-to-back chairs and workbaskets in the aisles. The 75-foot-long sewing machine tables stood in the way of those trying to reach windows, stairs, and elevators.

The firemen hauled a firehose up to the eighth floor. When they reached it, the fire "was so intense it was impossible to stand up. We lay down on our stomachs or on our knees to try to make an entrance." They put out the flames in less than 30 minutes, but in that time 146 died, mostly women and young girls. Hundreds were seriously burned. Thousands of family members spent days trying to identify their loved ones. Some could only be recognized by a shoe, ring, or scorched skirt. On the eighth and ninth floors, 24 wedding and engagement rings were found in the ashes.

Fire Chief Edward Croker found a mouse on the ninth floor. It was half drowned. He picked it up, stroked it, and then put it in his pocket. He told two firemen he would take it home. "It's alive," he said. "At least it's alive."

The Outrage

On April 5, 1911, some 120,000 workers from 60 trade unions held a funeral march for seven still-unidentified workers who died. It took almost three hours for marchers to pass the 400,000 spectators gathered to watch. The streets were draped with purple and black cloths, and businesses closed.

People were angry. Rallies were held. People had been dying in workplace fires for years. In 1910, there were 42 fires in shirtwaist factories alone. The emphasis had always been on building fireproof structures. And indeed the Asch Building was fireproof—it was still standing. But now everyone was determined to shift the focus. What about the people inside? How could they be kept safe? In February, 13,603 buildings had been listed as dangerous, but only 2,051 received follow-up inspections by the New York Fire Department.

Fire Chief Croker said, "It would be my advice to the girls employed in lofts and factories to refuse to work when they find the doors locked."

Dr. Anna Howard Shaw, a speaker at a rally at the Cooper Union on the Friday after the fire, said,

> There was a time when woman worked in the home with her weaving, her sewing, her candlemaking. All that has been changed. Now she can no longer regulate her own condition, her own hours of labor. She has been driven into the market with no voice in laws and powerless to defend herself. The most cowardly thing that men ever did was when they tied woman's hands and left her to be food for the flames.

New York City set up a commission to study the situation. The WTUL sent out a questionnaire to workers asking about their safety and used the anonymous responses to determine how many worked in a firetrap.

A 3,000-page report was then published that led to many changes. These included the requirement of fire alarms, fire drills, fire exits, fire escapes, and overhead sprinklers. People began to work harder to change child-labor laws. In 1913, a 54-hour workweek became the law. Many other changes were also made quickly. This New York model was followed around the country.

One witness to the Triangle fire, Frances Perkins, became a member of the investigating committee, along with Franklin D. Roosevelt, who was then a state senator. Later, when Roosevelt was elected president of the United States, he appointed her secretary of labor and the first woman cabinet member ever. This administration introduced many programs and laws for the benefit of the working poor and retired workers.

Who's to Blame?

The owners of the Triangle Shirtwaist Factory were Max Blanck and Isaac Harris. They were immigrants themselves, who became the "Shirtwaist Kings." They produced more shirtwaists than any other company. These fitted blouses, usually worn with a long skirt, were the height of fashion from 1895 to 1910 all over the United States. With magazines and catalogs now available everywhere, the entire nation could buy them. However, fashion was beginning to change as new ads came out for one-piece dresses. Divided skirts for riding bicycles were also becoming popular for ladies.

With all their profits, the Triangle Company could have installed sprinklers above the work floors for about $5,000. Nowadays if they did that, their insurance company would have rewarded them with reduced insurance rates—but not back then. The Triangle Company had no reason to make safety improvements because they could make plenty of money even if they had a fire.

By their own records, which were not well kept, the Triangle Company reported a stock of $134,075 worth of shirtwaists. The insurance company had allowed them to buy $199,750 worth of insurance and paid them that much after the fire. They made a profit of $64,950, or $445 for each worker who died. After the fire, they simply moved to another building and hired more contractors, who hired more girls eager to work.

The fire department knew that the Asch Building had only one inadequate fire escape and that there were only two narrow stairways, when three were required. They had overlooked these deficiencies and approved an inspection in 1911.

The people who built the Asch Building avoided a lot of safety regulations by making it only 135 feet tall. A 150-foot building required metal window frames and concrete floors. But at 135 feet they could save money with wood floors and wood window frames.

With an average of 136 workers a day, or 50,000 each year, dying in work-related accidents and fires in New York City, the people who lived there also bore some responsibility because they ignored the situation. Everyone down the line failed the shirtwaist makers in the Triangle Factory Fire.

In December 1911, the owners of the Triangle Factory were put on trial for manslaughter. They tried to promote their point of view with a million-dollar advertising campaign, but the

This narrow and inadequate staircase leading to the Triangle Factory passed an inspection before the fire. A wooden door at the top was often locked.

newpapers refused to run their ads. The judge instructed the jury to consider only three things:

1. Did the jury believe the doors were locked at all times?

2. Did the owners know they were locked?

3. Could the deaths have occurred if the doors had not been locked?

The all-male jury listened to 155 witnesses. The factory workers came dressed in their holiday best, but there were language problems and the prosecutor accused them of not telling the truth. The jury found the owners innocent.

The "Sweating System"

The "sweating system" started in the late 19th century, part of the change as people switched from doing work in their homes to gathering in a large work area. This was different from the "factory system." In a factory, the boss hires his own workers and everyone works together. In a sweating system, work is handed out to subcontractors, or "sweaters," usually immigrants themselves, who hire their own workers. The workers are frequently people they know, who speak their language. Often sweaters get entire families to work for them.

In 1891, Pope Leo XIII said, "A small number of very rich men have been able to lay upon the teeming masses of the laboring poor a yoke little better than slavery itself." Many saw factory workers as the new slaves.

A reporter for a magazine wrote, "A sweater's shop is a place where clothing is made for the big dealers at the prices that enable them to undersell their rivals and offer garments so wonderfully cheap, and it is in addition a graveyard for youth and hope."

Another wrote that "it is a place where the cost of a 'bargain' must be 'sweated' out of the workers."

Pauline Newman, who went to work at the Triangle Factory in 1901, wrote, "The corner of the shop would resemble a kindergarten because we were young, eight, nine, ten years old. . . . It was a world of greed; the human being didn't mean anything."

The "sweating system" traps workers because the manufacturer takes no responsibility for the wages that the sweater pays his employees. If workers ask for more money or benefits, he says, "I am paying you as much as I can from what I get from the manufacturer." If workers take their problem to the manufacturer (if they can find him), he says, "I am not responsible for what the sweater pays you. Talk to him." In the end, sweatshop workers often are not paid enough money to live on, even though they work long hours.

Sweatshops still exist today. They can be found in cities around the world with large immigrant communities. Any employer who ignores laws that define a minimum wage, age, and level of safety is running a sweatshop that violates the rights of workers.

In the United States, most sweatshops operating today are in the garment industry. Employees are usually immigrant women from Asia, Central America, and Mexico. The shops are dirty, dangerous, and cruel, and many are owned by immigrants. In 1995, in El Monte, California, 72 workers from Thailand were discovered trapped inside apartments; they were never let outside. They sewed clothes at least 17 hours a day, and sometimes up to 22 hours, earning about 69 cents an hour. They slept on the floor and were beaten regularly. They hoped their wages would pay off the $4,800 debt each owed for being brought to the United States.

How can these shops still exist? Manufacturers find they can keep prices low by sending orders to contractors who don't play by the rules. The employees are often illegal workers afraid that if they speak up they will be deported, sent back to their country, which they consider much worse than the sweatshop. And there are not enough inspectors to check 22,000 sewing businesses.

Sweatshops exist around the world. Millions of poor children must work to survive. Some live in families where the average yearly income is $500 per person or less. Some of them produce cheap clothing for chain stores right here in the United States. People who refuse to buy clothes made in sweatshops are taking action to support clothing made under safe, fair, and legal working conditions.

There are several ways to avoid clothing from sweatshops. Visit Green America's Responsible Shopper Web site to look up common stores, like Gap and TJ Maxx. A second Web site, National Green Pages, helps to identify artisans who sell directly to stores to earn a fair payment. When you are shopping, look for the UNITE label, which means the garment was made by members of UNITE HERE!, who have negotiated fair contracts with their companies. They have a Web site: www.unitehere.org. If you decide to change brands after some research, let the company know what they need to do to win you back as a customer.

CHAPTER SIX

Titanic

April 15, 1912

Crossing the Atlantic

More than a thousand years ago, Vikings crossed the Atlantic Ocean in open boats. Such daring! They risked being swamped or blown off course by fierce storms.

Covered sailing ships were an improvement, but they were also at the mercy of wind and waves, and the journey could take many weeks. Shipwrecks and mutinies were common. Seasick passengers brought their own food and used chamber pots for toilets, which were rarely emptied and added to the foul air. When they ran out of milk, children died. When they ran out of firewood, they couldn't cook and keep warm. If they had no fruits and vegetables, they developed a disease called scurvy. If they ran out of freshwater, everybody died.

When food was provided, few people had nice things to say about the quality. "The bread was full of worms and defiled with cockroaches." "Two bugs for every bean." In 1842, Charles Dickens, a famous English writer, described a first-class dining room as a "gigantic hearse with windows," where he was served "yellow boiled leg of mutton" and a "rather mouldy dessert."

As millions of immigrants wanted to make the Atlantic crossing in the late 1800s, steamships and ocean liners competed for this business by providing better service and faster speed. But a 1911 report, prepared by Anna Herkner for the Immigration Commission, still described a dire situation: "Immigrants lie in their berths for most of the voyage, in a stupor caused by the foul air. The food often repels them. . . . It is almost impossible to keep personally clean."

So in 1912, as the RMS *Titanic* prepared to take its first voyage from Southampton, England, to New York City, everyone paid attention. This new class of ocean liner was called a "floating palace at sea" with an emphasis on luxury similar to a five-star hotel. The ship had nine decks, where a crew of 899 would cater to the needs of over 1,300 passengers, some more pampered than others.

For a one-week voyage, 127,000 pieces of tableware were on board, along with 60 chefs and assistants, 40 tons of potatoes,

36,000 oranges, and 16,000 lemons. There was no chance any-one would get scurvy on this journey. The huge *Titanic* was fitted with so many comforts that it took three years and 15,000 men to build it.

The Shipbuilder's Art

A shipping company called the White Star Line hired Harland & Wolff in Belfast, Ireland, for the job. Thomas Andrews, chief designer, oversaw crews that worked on 26 boilers, each as tall as a house. Twenty horses were needed to haul in the main anchor. Three million rivets were used to hold the steel plates together. On the ship's sides steel rivets could be installed by newly invented hydraulic machines, but hand hammering was required on the curved bow. These rivets were made of a softer metal composed of wrought iron and slag. Unknown to the designers at the time, this change turned out to play a critical part in the story of the *Titanic*.

The amazing *Titanic* was built next to its sister ship, the *Olympic*. The construction was reported as "a new epoch in naval architecture" that made the vessel "practically unsink-able." Turbo engines were installed to provide extra power without using more coal. The hull had a double bottom and 15 compartments with watertight doors that could be closed instantly by "simply moving an electric switch." The walls of the compartments, however, did not extend all the way up to the next deck, leaving room at the top for water to overflow.

Eventually the ship was fitted with a grand staircase,

The life jackets were made of cork panels covered with thick canvas. They could keep people afloat but couldn't protect them from the icy cold.

elegant cabinets, elevators, restaurants, and the most powerful wireless Marconi telegraph system of the time. Seventy-five fans were installed to ensure that everyone had fresh air. Life jackets were provided for everyone, but the number of lifeboats was cut in half from the original 32 to free up extra deck space for walking. While 16 lifeboats complied with the English Board of Regulations, the regulations hadn't been updated for the new large ships. Later, four extra collapsible lifeboats were added, but there were still only enough seats for about half of the 2,200 people aboard.

White Star planned much of its marketing to attract wealthy Americans. The *Titanic* was described as "eloquent testimony to the progress of mankind . . . the movement of the British and American people towards the ideal of international and universal peace." More than a ship, it was a salute to innovation and engineering in an era much like today—everyone was proud of new technology and rushed to buy the latest inventions.

Captain Edward J. Smith was chosen to take command of the ship. He had 24 years of experience as a captain and was a favorite of wealthy passengers and crews who had sailed with him before. Smith had total confidence in the ability of modern shipbuilding to avoid disaster, as did most people who signed up eagerly for the maiden journey. One deckhand told a passenger, "God himself could not sink this ship."

Before the *Titanic* could begin its journey, a strike by British coal miners left the new liner scrambling for fuel. The crew managed to "pirate" 4,427 tons from six ships idled by the strike. After loading, some coal caught fire and simmered for three days, warping a steel wall between compartments. Soon the ship had a much bigger problem. The "unsinkable" *Titanic* was about to become the biggest disaster in the history of Atlantic crossings.

Pampered to the Last

On the *Titanic*, first class was opulent. Rich and famous passengers paid at least $400 (the equivalent of $5,000 today) for a ticket, and some paid as much as $3,300. John Jacob Astor, the fur trader's great-grandson and a powerful businessman who built luxury hotels, bought tickets for himself, his wife, her maid, his manservant, and Kitty, their Airedale dog. A famous fashion designer, a mystery writer, a tennis star, the director of Quaker Oats, and a friend of President Taft with a message from the pope were also among the first class. The owners of the ship emphasized that the *Titanic* offered both "beneficial exercise, besides endless amusement." First-class passenger Lady Duff-Gordon called the *Titanic* a "floating palace" for a "small world bent on pleasure."

First-class travelers enjoyed a gymnasium, squash courts, Turkish baths, two barbershops, three elevators, and eight musicians. They also had exclusive use of the Café Parisien, which, according to the *Southampton Times*, had a "charming, sun-lit verandah, tastefully decorated in French trellis-work with ivy and other creeping plants." The seven children in this group were allowed to swim in the pool and use the gym, where they could ride a wooden horse. A smoking room was for men only.

On Sunday night, April 14, many in first class dined at the Ritz restaurant. Mrs. Walter Douglas said, "The tables were gay with pink roses and white daisies, the women in their beautiful shimmering gowns of satin and silk, the men immaculate. . . . The food was superb: caviar, lobster, quail from Egypt, plover's eggs, and hothouse grapes and fresh peaches."

Second class was more than comfortable. These passengers paid an average of $65 for a ticket, to share an elevator, library, smoking room, and the boat deck. Many of these travelers were teachers, engineers, and other professionals, and 27 kids were in this group. They liked the "natural light in each cabin" and food "better than home." On Sunday night, they enjoyed a menu from the same kitchen as first class but with fewer choices.

Third class, also called steerage, consisted mostly of immigrants leaving Europe and the Middle East. Tickets averaged $35, and these passengers brought very little luggage. There were 89 children in this group. Speaking many languages, third-class passengers enjoyed a general room and a smoking room and were allowed to use the windy rear deck that caught smoky discharge from the ship's boilers. Their beds were comfortable, but 700 people shared two baths. They ate in shifts because there were only 473 seats. On Sunday they ate a midday dinner of soup, stew, biscuits, potatoes, and desserts served on linen tablecloths. Later they could have tea and biscuits. For those escaping from poverty, persecution, and war, this was luxury.

Warning! Icebergs!

Earlier, on Sunday morning, the *Titanic* had received a telegram: "West-bound steamers report bergs, growlers, and field ice." It was the season when thousands of icebergs calved off the Greenland glacier, and some drifted south into the sea lanes. By 2 P.M., with four more ice warnings, the captain shifted course 10 miles farther south. Two men were in the crow's nest on lookout. In spite of all the opulent supplies on this floating palace, they had no binoculars.

By dinnertime, the air was bitter cold. At 7:30 P.M., a message from the freighter *Californian* warned of three icebergs. This didn't reach the captain, who was eating lobster and caviar with a group of first-class passengers.

At nine o'clock, the captain made an appearance on the bridge. He ordered a top speed of 26 miles per hour—"slow down only if hazy." Was he trying to make a fast crossing? The chairman of White Star, Bruce Ismay, was overheard urging him to "beat the *Olympic*" in their crossing time. Passengers who checked the daily mileage posted outside the purser's office were pleased to discover that the ship had traveled 546

The largest part of an iceberg is underwater. When the Titanic *hit the iceberg, the collision caused steel plates to buckle and rivets to pop. Great volumes of water flooded into five compartments, too many for the "unsinkable" ship to stay afloat.*

miles in the last 24 hours and had not yet fired up her last two boilers.

At 10:55 P.M., senior radio operator Jack Phillips received another iceberg warning from the *Californian*: "We are stopped and surrounded by ice." Jack was already overwhelmed with messages coming from a distant station and did not welcome the interruption from a nearby vessel. "Keep out! Shut up! I am busy," he telegraphed and put the warning aside. Soon Jack would be relieved by junior operator Harold Bride, but there was only one operator on the *Californian*. The *Californian* operator closed the wireless room and went to bed at 11.30 P.M. During the next critical hours, this ship missed all urgent messages from the *Titanic*.

In the crow's nest, lookout Frederick Fleet strained to see through the moonless night. Because the sea was unusually calm, there were no white ripples sloshing against icebergs. He spotted "a small, dark mass" in the distance. As the ship got closer, he realized it was enormous. At 11:40 he struck the warning bell and telephoned the bridge. "Iceberg right ahead," he yelled.

Mr. William Murdoch, officer of the watch, telegraphed the engine room: "Hard-a-starboard. Stop. Full speed astern." For a brief moment it looked like the ship would clear the iceberg. But they had only 37 seconds and the 882-foot liner was going too fast to make the turn.

An Icy Collision

The *Titanic* grazed the ice on the starboard side. In less than 10 seconds, the iceberg popped the weak rivets and created holes below the waterline. Clumps of ice crashed to the deck, and passengers started to kick pieces around like soccer balls. In the kitchen below, a night baker watched a pan of fresh rolls clatter to the floor. But many hardly noticed. "It did not seem to me there was any great impact at all. It was as though we went over about a thousand marbles," said Mrs. Stuart White. Mrs. Walter Stephenson, who had survived the 1906 San Francisco earthquake, said, "This jolt wasn't so bad." Men playing cards didn't step outside to look. Thomas Andrews, the designer, was so involved in sketching improvements for the ship that he didn't leave his room. But on the bridge, First Officer Murdoch quickly pulled the lever to close the watertight doors.

On the lowest decks, the engineers and stokers heard a "tremendous noise." A carpenter reported water gushing in, and

Sea biscuits (sometimes called hardtack) are thick crackers used as survival food. Sea biscuits were placed on every lifeboat but many survivors, who had never been drilled on lifeboat safety, did not discover them.

so did a mail clerk. Andrews was called out of his room to make an inspection with Captain Smith and found five compartments filling with water. Andrews made some quick calculations with terror on his face. The captain looked pale when told the *Titanic* would sink in about two hours. Quickly he ordered the lifeboats uncovered, and the bakers brought bread and water to the boats.

At 12:15 A.M., Harold Bride tapped out CQD, CQD, a signal for distress. He gave their position so rescue ships could find them. Then he switched to SOS, SOS, a new distress signal that was easier to tap. The signals were picked up by ships in the area, but the closest one, *Californian,* with its wireless room shut down for the night, didn't get the message. David Sarnoff, a radio hobbyist in New York, became the main source of information. Messages got scrambled, and rumors were wild. On Monday, the New York *Evening Sun* reported that the *Titanic* was being towed to Halifax.

The *Carpathia* heard the signal, and its captain, Arthur Henry Rostron, gave orders to head toward the *Titanic*, which was 60 miles away. While they steered around icebergs, the ship doctors went on standby, dining rooms were converted into hospitals, food and supplies were prepared, and rockets were fired every 15 minutes to alert other ships. Rostron estimated he could reach the *Titanic* in about four hours. But those on the "ship without peer in the ocean" didn't have that much time.

Women and Children First?

At 12:25 A.M., the crew was told to awaken passengers and instruct them to put on the life jackets that were available for all. Some people did not want to wear them, and those already in their nightclothes preferred to stay in their warm cabins. "This ship could smash a hundred icebergs and not feel it," said one. Just in case, a few anxious passengers rushed to the purser's office to claim valuables.

While the musicians played ragtime and dance tunes, some didn't get informed. "Not a single warning was given in the part of the ship in which I was. . . . We could have died like rats in a trap," said Mrs. George Stone, who was in first class. Third-class passengers, who were in the bottom levels, had a hard time making their way to the upper deck, and some reported that closed gates keeping them from first- and second-class areas remained locked.

At 12:45 A.M., the *Titanic* started to fire distress rockets. The captain and some of the crew and passengers spotted a ship in the distance, a four-masted freighter with one funnel, which might have been the *Californian*. The ship never responded.

While engineers and electricians worked hard to keep the

pumps and lights going, lifeboat 7 was lowered. Only 28 of 60 seats were filled. Lifeboat 1 (capacity for 40) was lowered with only five first-class passengers and seven crew members. One of them, Sir Cosmo Duff-Gordon, gave money to the lifeboat crew. This act later fueled a great controversy. Was the money a kindness or a bribe to obtain an exclusive lifeboat? Several other lifeboats were also lowered with empty seats, partly because many doubted they were in serious danger and expected the ship on the horizon to come to the rescue. Also, the crew hadn't been drilled, and some of them thought it might be unsafe to lower a full boat.

The captain gave the order to load women and children first and told some lifeboat crews to row for the ship in the distance and then return for more passengers. On one side of the ship, men were allowed into lifeboats. On the other side, they were not, and an officer used pistols to turn them away. When Mr. Isidor Straus, founder of Macy's in New York, was not allowed into a lifeboat, his wife, Ida, chose to stay with him.

Ruth Becker, a second-class passenger, age 12, managed to find her way through the great maze of the ship and help her mother, younger brother, and sister get into lifeboat 11. There was no room for her, but eventually an officer dropped her into lifeboat 13. Lady Charlotte Cardeza persuaded Murdoch to allow her 37-year-old son and his valet to join her in lifeboat 3. Wealthy businessman Benjamin Guggenheim and his manservant could not get seats. They changed into formal evening clothes. "We're dressed up in our best and are prepared to go down like gentlemen," said Guggenheim. Third-class passenger Alfred Rush had just turned 16 and was proudly wearing long trousers for the first time. When offered a chance to get into a lifeboat, he held back and said, "No, I'm staying here with the men." Toward the end, children were given no preference, and some as young as nine were denied a seat as the situation grew desperate and all realized the ship was sinking.

At two o'clock that morning, freezing seawater lapped onto the boat deck, where only two lifeboats remained. Some threw deck chairs overboard and jumped in. A group went below to play a last hand of cards. Others prayed. The musicians kept playing. The lights were still burning. In the final moments, a man traveling under the name Mr. Hoffman managed to get his two young sons into the last boat, though he was not

Michel, age three, and Edmond Navratil, age two, had been kidnapped by their father and were traveling under fake names. They survived, but their father did not. Eventually, they were reunited with their mother in France.

allowed in. Later, these boys were discovered to have been kidnapped from their mother in France and were returned to her.

At 2:18 A.M., the bow was low, the stern high. Furniture, pianos, plates, and cargo tumbled loudly through the tilting vessel. Lights blinked and then went out. The ship cracked and broke apart. The *Titanic* spiraled down, down, to the cold depths of the Atlantic, and 1,500 people were doomed without a lifeboat.

Rescue

The glassy sea was littered with deck chairs, crates, and people thrashing in 28-degree water. Only lifeboats 4 and 14 returned for a rescue effort. They saved 13, but three died later from the cold. Cries and moans were heard for 20 minutes, then all was quiet. Those in the water died from hypothermia, slipping quickly into a cold sleep. Mrs. Dodge from San Francisco was so angered by her boat's refusal to help those in the water that she and her four-year-old son made a precarious move to lifeboat 7 when it approached.

Mrs. James J. Brown, a millionaire from the Colorado gold rush, was in lifeboat 6 (65 seats but only 30 aboard). She wrapped her sable stole around the legs of a shivering stoker and did not like a crewman's order to sit quietly and do nothing. So she took over, showed the women in the boat how to row, and headed them toward the ship in the distance that the rowers were unable to overtake. She later became known as "unsinkable Molly Brown."

At 4:00 A.M., the *Carpathia* arrived. With chattering teeth and frozen hair, *Titanic* survivors burned newspaper and handkerchiefs to be seen. By then the lifeboats were spread over a four-mile area and it took four hours to get them aboard. Some weren't strong enough to climb a steep ladder, so they were pulled up in a boatswain's chair. Children were scooped up in mail sacks. At 8:20 P.M., the captain sent a telegram. Finally friends and relatives waiting for accurate news knew of the sinking.

In all, 706 people were rescued, and over 1,500 were lost. If

After spending over four hours on the icy Atlantic, survivors finally reached the Carpathia. Life jackets were available to all, but not everybody wore one.

all lifeboat seats had been filled, an additional 500 people could have been saved. Because of terrible weather, the rest of the crossing to New York took four days, and 40,000 people were gathered at the dock to meet the survivors. In Southampton (home of 699 of the 899 crew members, including the captain), relatives and friends waited outside the White Star office to hear the news from across the ocean.

Harold Bride, the junior telegraph operator, survived but suffered from frostbite and injured feet. He agreed to be carried to the wireless room to help the exhausted operator on the *Carpathia*, who was overwhelmed with messages.

Captain Smith did not survive. Thomas Andrews and John Jacob Astor did not survive. All the musicians perished. Only 24 percent of the crew and 25 percent of third class survived, but 42 percent of second class and 62 percent of first class were rescued. Helen Lorraine Allison, age two, was the only first-class child who did not survive. All second-class children survived, but only 32 of the 89 steerage children made it into a lifeboat.

People were shocked to see that a "whim of nature," as poet Thomas Hardy described it, could destroy such a magnificent ship as the *Titanic*. The sinking caused them to doubt man's ability to conquer everything. Just when man thought nothing could go wrong, it did.

Down, Down, to the Bottom of the Sea

Many survivors put in claims for what they had lost. Lady Cardeza in first class used 18 pages to list items in 14 trunks,

4 bags, a jewel case, and a packing case, for a total value of $177,352.75. Eugene Daly in third class claimed a "set of bagpipes, $50." Molly Brown's claim included $500 for three crates of ancient artifacts that she had collected for the Denver Museum. Ruth Becker's list included "6 cambric gowns with hand made lace, $28." Others made claims for $100,000 for an oil painting; $3,000 for "a picture of Garibaldi, signed by him and presented to my grandfather"; $750 for a champion French bulldog named Gamin de Pycombe; $50 for "handwritten college lecture notes, 2 year course"; $5,000 for one "Renault 25 hp automobile"; and one million dollars for loss of life of Henry B. Harris, theater magnate.

Claims were filed in both the United States and Britain, but the process was very slow. Everything was further delayed when paperwork was sent on the *Lusitania* during World War I. This ship was torpedoed by a German submarine and sank. After more delays and investigations, $663,000 was distributed to all involved, about 4 percent of the $17 million claimed.

Survivors from the crew lost everything but the clothes they were wearing. Home was far away across the ocean. When inquiries into the sinking were held in Washington, D.C., some of the crew were paid expenses to testify, but for all of them, their wages ceased at 2:20 A.M., April 15, 1912, when the ship sank. Eventually they were sent home by White Star and had to rely on emergency shipwreck payments from the Sailor's Union until they could find another job. Hundreds of sailors refused to sail on *Olympic* and other large ships until the issue of insufficient lifeboats could be resolved.

Most in third class lost everything they owned. White Star provided temporary shelter for them. Relatives of the musicians were sent a bill for lost uniforms, and 75 percent of their pay was deducted because they had not completed the round-trip terms of their contract.

Iceberg Alley

Brian T. Hill, from the Institute for Ocean Technology in Canada, has compiled a list and map locations of ships besides *Titanic* that have collided with icebergs. He has found more than 600 ships, including eight traveling on their first voyage. Each year, 40,000 icebergs calve off Greenland, and hundreds drift south into the shipping lanes. Their size is hard to judge because most of the volume is underwater. What sailors see is only the tip of the iceberg, and *Titanic* was only one of thousands of ships that have taken a perilous journey through Iceberg Alley.

Scientists have been analyzing the iceberg problem for years. An idea to get rid of them didn't work. In 1959, the U.S. Coast Guard pummeled an iceberg with 3,600 kilograms of bombs in an effort to blow it up. The iceberg only tilted slightly. Ice is extremely hard. In a collision, ice that has been hit melts and then refreezes in the blink of an eye. In that quick action, it absorbs the massive energy of a collision. Steel crumples, and ice ends up with a bit of scraped paint on it.

Before the *Titanic* sank, safety was considered part of good design. After the collision, lifeboats and messages also became vitally important. Today ships must assign lifeboat seats for all passengers and crew, regardless of the class of ticket, and hold weekly lifeboat drills. Twenty-four-hour radio service is also required, along with hourly "listen out" periods when messages are stopped to give distress calls priority.

After the sinking, U.S. and British ships started daily patrols to report on ice conditions. In 1914, 13 North Atlantic nations set up the International Ice Patrol to scout for icebergs. Today ships, airplanes, satellites, and buoys monitor drifting ice. All icebergs are logged and reported to ships making the Atlantic crossing. For extra safety, ships are required to travel farther south during the iceberg season.

Sunken Treasure and Rusticles

As stories swirled of gold, silver, and jewels that went down with the *Titanic*, many searched for the shipwreck. Because they couldn't find it, adventurers wondered if it had been buried in a severe underwater earthquake in 1929. Or had it rotted away? Or did someone manage to raise the *Titanic*?

Those early searches were based on the location tapped out in the CQD message from 1912. Finally, in the 1980s, Robert D. Ballard from the Woods Hole Oceanographic Institution did further research. He recalculated a possible new location and traveled deep in a submersible that took him where no light could reach and where fish had "bodies

Captain Smith's bathtub can be seen two and a half miles under the sea. As in the rest of the great ship, rusticles are growing all around and slowly munching up the steel.

totally white, their immense purple eyes apparently blind." After 56 days of searching, a boiler from the *Titanic* was spotted, then the ship itself. It was in two pieces, two and a half miles below the surface. Worms had eaten away some of the wood, but much was preserved. Over the years, thousands of artifacts have been removed, including silk socks, a wool jacket, four London omnibus tickets, a white cotton work shirt with red stripes, a milk warmer with the White Star logo, a second-class soup tureen, portholes, leather bags, a glass bottle filled with olives, and tons of coal. An agreement was reached to preserve these items for historical research and public viewing, which has caused some controversy because the shipwreck is a gravesite.

The shipwreck itself has turned into the largest known collection of organisms on earth. Tiny microbes have been munching *Titanic* iron and dangle from the wreck like rusty icicles. They are living communities of bacteria and fungi called "rusticles." Worms live with them, burrowing through the tissues and eating bacterial waste. Eventually rusticles will remove all iron from the *Titanic* as they slowly recycle 24,000 tons of steel back to nature.

Since the sinking, the world population has increased by over four billion, and more people than ever are fascinated by the oral histories, unlikely heroes, and unsolved mysteries of this event. There are thousands of Web pages on the subject. "Tip of the iceberg," "the band played on," "women and children first," and "every man for himself" are old sayings that have become widely associated with this ship. While the rusticles munch, the *Titanic* story continues to grow as a most unforgettable disaster of man in nature.

The sunken Titanic *was finally located after 80 years under the sea. Thousands of artifacts were recovered, including an intact jar of olives.*

CHAPTER SEVEN

Blue Skin and Bloody Sputum

Pandemic Flu of 1918

I had a little bird
And its name was Enza.
I opened the window
and in-flew-Enza.

In 1918, children started to sing this new jump-rope song. It was about influenza, flu for short, a sickness that was killing people everywhere. No one understood the cause, no one could find an effective cure, and it seemed to spread as easily as opening the window.

Today scientists know much more about flu, but they still don't know how to stop it completely. Every winter, tricky flu viruses get into people's lungs and cause terrible muscle aches, chills, and coughing; this usually lasts about 10 days. In the United States, about 36,000 people die each year, and up to 500,000 deaths occur worldwide. These victims are usually the very old, the very young, or those already weak with another illness.

But the 1918 strain of flu virus was 25 times more deadly than ordinary flu. Half of the people in the world got it, and it is estimated that at least 50 million died. Many victims were between 20 and 30 years old, an unusual age for flu fatalities. Young soldiers died. Young parents died, leaving children behind. In New York City alone, 21,000 children were orphaned.

When an epidemic spreads this widely and kills so easily, it is called a deadly pandemic. The pandemic of 1918 killed more people in a few months than any other illness in the history of the world. Today medical researchers are working hard to understand what made this flu strain so lethal. With other kinds of flu viruses still infecting us, it is an extremely important question. No one knows for sure where the 1918 strain came from or how it turned into such a killer. Jeffery Taubenberger, a medical researcher, said, "Here was a mass murderer . . . who's never been brought to justice. And what we're trying to do is find the murderer."

The First Wave of the Killer Flu

The Pandemic Flu of 1918 occurred during World War I, when most of Europe and its allies were fighting against Germany and its allies. After three years of war, millions had already died from the newest weapons—machine guns that could fire 80 shots per minute, mustard gas with its deadly green haze, tanks, submarines, and shells that could hit long-distance targets. With new fighting methods, soldiers were digging trenches and living belowground.

Troops were vaccinated and deloused for protection against some diseases. But there was no protection from the flu. During the war, soldiers and sailors were jammed into camps, tents, ships, and submarines. Farm boys mixed with city boys, each with "entirely different disease immunities and vulnerabilities," wrote John Barry. Civilians flooded into densely populated cities in the rush to make war materials. Workers sometimes shared the same bed in shifts. They shared cups, forks, and outhouses. At times they gathered in huge patriotic groups to buy war bonds and support the troops. Crowded and stressed, they were easy targets for a virus.

The first wave of flu began in the spring of 1918. At Fort Riley, Kansas, soldiers began to stumble in to the hospital with headaches and sore throats. By the end of the week, 522 were sick and 48 had died. Meanwhile, 80,000 soldiers, some of them from Fort Riley, were rushed off to Europe to help England and France defend against a strong German attack. Men began dying of the flu as the transport ships crossed the

Atlantic Ocean. Others made it off the ships, then spread the sickness to new areas. Soldiers visiting families back in the United States carried the flu to the cities, and great numbers of workers and students started to call in sick.

The epidemic spread across Europe. In Spain, eight million were sick, including King Alfonso XIII. Spain was not at war and had no press censorship, so most early reports of the flu came from there. As a result, it is sometimes called the Spanish flu. Sometimes it is called the three-day fever because that

The flu spread quickly during wartime as people, such as these marines, were crowded together on ships and then transported to faraway places.

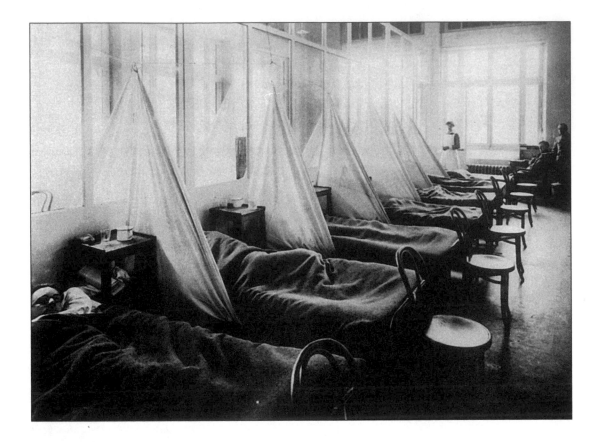

As the flu spread through Europe, this crowded army hospital in France hung sheets between beds in a further effort to stop the disease.

was about how long the sickness lasted. For those who did not recover, death came quickly, in 24 to 48 hours.

Some Americans suspected the Germans of using a killer microbe as a biological weapon. In fact, many became suspicious of every German or Austrian in the United States. But the Germans were getting sick too. They called it Flanders Fever. As the sickness spread through German troops, it slowed down an attack that was their last real chance to win the war. The battle plan was postponed daily, and the German commander, Erich Ludendorff, wrote that it was difficult to listen every morning to the chiefs of staff as they reported on the "number of influenza cases and their complaints about the weakness of their troops."

The flu affected the other side too. King George of England got sick, and so did 10,313 of his sailors. For three weeks, the British Grand Fleet was unable to go to sea. A British army division had to put off a planned attack in June when too many soldiers got sick.

There were no quarantines, and the virus traveled through China and Japan along shipping and railroad lines. But this first wave barely touched Africa, South America, and Canada. In August, the British army and a medical journal stated that the epidemic had disappeared, and everyone gave a sigh of relief.

But the flu pandemic wasn't over. And through a mysterious process that medical researchers today are still trying to understand, when it reappeared, it emerged like nothing the world had ever seen before.

The Second Wave: Blue Skin and Bloody Sputum

In August, just as everyone was rejoicing that the flu was gone, the second wave hit, and it was no longer a three-day fever. This deadly strain broke out at three port cities at once, on three different continents separated by thousands of miles of ocean. Sick people had new symptoms—blue skin and bloody sputum. Victims were struck so suddenly that they toppled off horses or collapsed in the kitchen. They

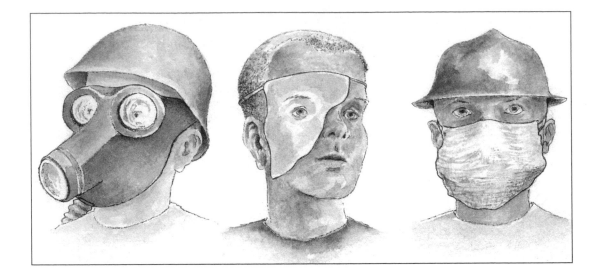

Soldiers wore masks in World War I: gas masks to protect from poison, carefully painted face masks to hide injuries, and gauze masks to protect from flu.

gasped for breath like they were drowning. Some died quickly, while walking down the street or just as they arrived at the hospital.

In Africa, at Freetown, Sierra Leone, the disease was so contagious that two-thirds of the town got sick. On August 27, when the HMS *Africa* pulled into the port for a load of coal, most of the laborers for the Sierra Leone Coaling Company were too sick to work. The ship's crew helped to load the coal. Within a few weeks, nearly 600 of the crew members were sick, and 51 died. A New Zealand transport ship carrying troops to the war front also stopped at the port. Soon 900 of the 1,150 crew members were sick, and 38 died.

About the same time, so many French soldiers stationed at Brest, France, were sick with flu and pneumonia that the navy hospital was forced to close. On August 19, the *New York Times* noted, "A considerable number of American negroes, who have gone to France on horse transports, have contracted Spanish influenza on shore and died in French hospitals of pneumonia." Flu victims often developed pneumonia or other bacterial infections in their weakened lungs. Some died from the flu, others from infections that followed. As troops from all over the world trained at Brest and then went to war, the virus traveled with them.

Meanwhile, in Boston, Massachusetts, an overcrowded barrack for 7,000 soldiers started to fill its hospital with sick men. The doctors isolated the sick, tried to find a vaccine, and began to use prisoners for experiments, but they couldn't stop the disease. The citizens of Boston started to get sick and then the virus made its way to overcrowded Camp Devens, just outside Boston. When the flu arrived, a doctor known only by his first name, Roy, recorded his alarm: "It was the most vicious type of Pneumonia that has ever been seen. Two hours after admission they have the Mahogany spots over the cheek bones." Dr. Victor Vaughan was also horrified: "Their faces soon wear a bluish cast; a distressing cough brings up the blood-stained sputum. In the morning the dead bodies are stacked about the morgue like cord wood."

The victims' skin turned blue because their sick lungs were no longer able to transfer oxygen into the blood. Because their bodies turned dark, some thought this sickness must be the Black Death. Victims had nosebleeds, and their hands became numb and clumsy. Sometimes pockets of air formed under their skin and crackled. Some people even became delusional.

Camp Devens was experiencing 100 deaths every day, with many dying in just a few hours. With so many bodies, specially equipped trains were used to carry them away. The Red Cross, overwhelmed with sick people in Boston, managed to send 12 nurses to help. Eight of them got sick, and two died. The hospital, built for 1,200, overflowed with 8,000 patients. Many were unattended. "No one ever took our temperature and I never even saw a doctor," said a patient. Autopsies performed on some who died revealed lungs filled with bloody froth. Flu victims drowned in their own body fluids.

A quarantine was finally ordered, but it was too late. A steamer had already left Boston for New Orleans and then traveled on to Mexico, spreading the illness. Another ship set out for Philadelpia, and in one terrible week in that city 4,500 died of the flu. As soldiers were transferred to Chicago, Seattle, and other areas, the flu followed. The United States was forced to cancel a draft for 142,000 new soldiers. Still, soldiers continued to be transferred to other camps. In the cities, public health directors, reluctant to interfere with the war effort or to frighten citizens, were slow to close schools and impose quarantines.

The flu continued to spread around the world. Many died quickly, including doctors and nurses. Medical students were expected to act as doctors and, when possible, provide fluids and food for the sick. Fire, police, garbage, and telephone services were chaotic. Funerals were limited to 15 minutes or banned altogether, and people fought over the last of the coffins.

Gauze Masks and Raw Onions

With no cures available, many measures were tried to stop the pandemic. Many cities passed laws requiring people to cover their mouth and nose with gauze masks made by volunteers. "Obey the laws and wear the gauze. Protect your jaws from septic paws" was the advice given by public health officials in San Francisco and San Diego. "Mask slackers" were fined and jailed if they did not wear them. But viruses are such small organisms, a thousand times smaller than bacteria. Wearing a mask did no good; it was like expecting a tennis racket to hold a handful of sand.

Like this group in Seattle, people around the country wore masks in an effort to avoid the flu. However, even if the masks were worn correctly, covering both the mouth and nose, the microscopic virus could pass through the gauze material.

Parents tried many homemade remedies to keep the flu away from their children, including tying bags of camphor, an insect repellent, around their necks.

Posters encouraged people not to cough, spit, or sneeze. SPITTING EQUALS DEATH was one message. Soldiers were required to spray their throats with antiseptic or alcohol. Some were told to chew tobacco. Sheets were hung between patients to snare germs. Vaccines were created, but since they did not contain the flu virus, none of them worked.

Without a medical solution, people came up with their own ideas. One woman fed her children raw onions. Others tried spinach, turnips, or flaxseed. Some carried potatoes in their pockets or tied cucumber slices to their shoes. "Spanish Infuenza Remedy" was sold in Chicago, and a turbaned snake charmer was hired to attract attention. In New Orleans a chant was used: "Sour, sour, vinegar V, keep the sickness off of me." One doctor even suggested the removal of tonsils and teeth.

On September 21, the *Philadelphia Inquirer* announced that the cause had been found. It was a bacterium called Pfeiffer's bacillus, named after the scientist who discovered the germ 20 years earlier. Bacteria are much larger than viruses, and microscopes of the time could bring them into view. Pfeiffer's bacillus was detected in the lungs of some flu victims, but it turned out to be a false clue. It was just that the flu made it easier for the bacteria to infect the lungs. The real culprit, flu virus, could not be seen and then studied until the powerful electron microscope was invented in the 1930s. However, lung tissue samples were taken from victims and carefully preserved in paraffin. Then they were sent to a government warehouse for long-term storage.

The war ended on November 11, 1918. This was a great day of rejoicing around the United States and Europe, and crowds were out dancing and kissing in the streets. But the flu was not over. Many men who survived the war died of the flu as a third wave swept the globe, touching nearly every remote corner except American Samoa, where a strict quarantine had been enforced. When it reached 80 Inuits living in igloos in Brevig Mission, Alaska, only three adults and five children survived. The dead were buried in permafrost, and some became frozen mummies with preserved tissues.

Eighty years later, better research techniques allowed Jeffery Taubenberger to learn more about the deadly pandemic of 1918. He looked for genetic material in the lung tissue stored in paraffin at the government warehouse. He also looked at lung tissue from a mummified body from Brevig Mission. He was very persistent and finally discovered enough about the genetic code to realize that the flu of 1918 started in birds and then infected humans without making a lot of changes. The virus may have been so new that humans had no immunity. Since then, medical researchers have continued to unravel mysteries of the flu virus. Everyone wants to understand the 1918 flu to allow better prevention and control over any possible new pandemic.

A Tricky Parasite

Today scientists know that flu viruses are tricky, costume-changing parasites. They can look one way for a time and then mutate into a new look. Antibodies made by a human immune system to fight off one flu virus may not recognize the next version because it looks a bit different. This is why people can get the flu more than once. It is possible to build up some immunity, but not total immunity, total protection from a flu virus that has shifted into a new look.

Flu viruses don't infect the whole body. They head for the lung cells and carry two types of proteins to help them drill right in. These proteins stick out on the virus like tiny spears. One protein, hemagglutinin (shortened to H), helps the virus attach to a lung cell. The other protein, neuraminidase (shortened to N), provides the slippery mucus to slide in. The H and N proteins are the "costume changers," so each virus is described by the H and N proteins involved. The "Asian flu" of 1957 was H2N2. The "Hong Kong flu" of 1968 was H3N2. Those two epidemics together killed about two million people. The flu in 1918 was H1N1. This is the combination of proteins that killed more military people in the 20th century than all those who died in World War I, World War II, the Korean War, and the Vietnam War combined.

After the flu died back in 1919, people rarely talked about it. They seemed more interested in rebuilding postwar lives than in worrying about a sickness that left no physical reminders, such as pock marks. Forty-three thousand military people died of the flu, but their families didn't feel as proud as those whose relatives died of war injuries. Encyclopedias and history books barely mentioned it. Few articles or books were written about it. Memories of the deadly pandemic faded for all except the medical researchers who continued to study it. They experimented on themselves, pigs, ferrets, mice, guinea pigs, and prisoners, who were given a pardon for participation. They learned that pigs started to get the flu in the fall of 1918. Pigs probably caught the H1N1 strain from humans at the Cedar Rapids Swine Show in Iowa. Sometimes humans can catch the flu from pigs, but this time it seems the pigs caught it from humans. As viruses go from humans to animals and back again, these connections are very important for understanding how tricky little flu parasites can become so deadly.

The Bird/Pig Connection

Birds get the flu. Chickens with bird flu can die quickly, in a matter of hours. Wild birds, on the other hand, can travel around with up to 15 strains of flu virus in their gut and not look or act sick. People usually cannot catch the flu from birds the way they can from pigs.

Pigs can be a host to both bird flu and human flu viruses. If an unlucky pig should catch both bird flu and human flu at the same time, then the viruses can get remixed in the pig. As the H and N proteins shift, the result can be a new bird flu virus that can infect humans. People would not have immunity to it, although a 2007 study by Dr. Richard Webby suggests that yearly flu shots may offer weak protection against H5N1 bird flu. "It's not going to prevent infection," said Dr. Webby. "But it might reduce the more severe parts of the disease."

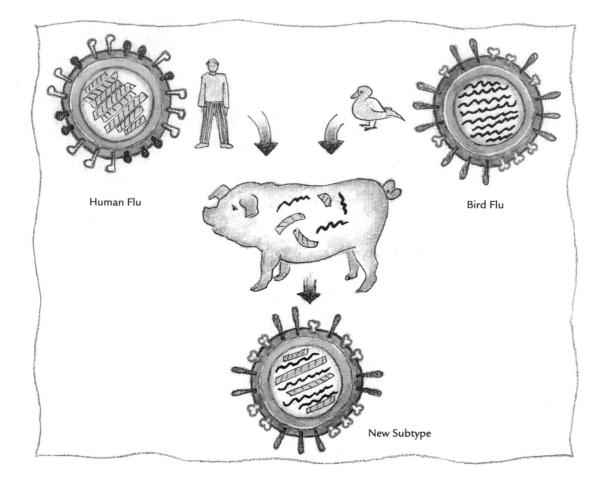

Human Flu

Bird Flu

New Subtype

The pig is a "mixer." If it should catch both a human flu and a bird flu, the result could be a new type of flu. The flu virus in 1918, however, went straight from birds to people. Scientists today are concerned about any new flu and especially any bird flu that people catch directly.

The epidemics of 1957 and 1968 started in birds and then were remixed in pigs. Both were first seen in an area of China where millions of people, and billions of chickens and pigs, all live close together. There are plenty of opportunities for the bird, pig, and human viruses to mix. This area is also a stopover for migrating birds and has become a prime spot for new epidemics to emerge. Major epidemics occur every 30 or 40 years, and a new swine flu virus emerged in 2009.

But the pandemic flu of 1918 was different. Scientists recently discovered that this flu virus occurred first in birds and then went straight to people. Pigs did not serve as a mixing pot for the H1N1 strain. With this information, scientists are on the lookout for any new flu virus that comes directly from birds, as it has the potential to be very deadly.

Unfortunately, a new bird flu, H5N1, has been popping up in Asia since 1997. It is responsible for the deaths of millions of chickens and over 100 people, but so far it has not met all three conditions necessary to become a deadly pandemic. One, it must start in an animal so that it appears new to humans, who will have no immunity. H5N1 is definitely new. Two, it must have the ability to make people sick. People do get very sick with the new bird flu. Three, it must be very easy for people to catch. So far, the new flu is not easy for people to catch, but scientists continue to monitor it carefully and have found some medical surprises.

Tigers and Other New Animal Connections

In 2003, Bengal tigers in Thailand started to get sick and die of the H5N1 strain of bird flu. They had been eating raw chicken for years, and this was the first time they had ever gotten sick. Researchers were alarmed that the strain had shifted into a form that could infect a new animal. The H5N1 strain was also infecting other animals and birds that never

Around the world, scientists are monitoring birds, both wild and domestic, for signs of illness.

had it before, including pheasants, black swans, clouded leopards, mice, cats, eagles, and storks.

Before 1997, not even farmers who handled sick birds every day became ill with bird flu. But on May 21, 1997, a three-year-old boy in Hong Kong died from H5N1 strain. He had eaten a pudding made with raw chicken blood. In December, several more people became ill. To stop the disease, every chicken in Hong Kong was killed. All was quiet until 2003, when people started to get bird flu again. Hundreds of millions of animals in nearly a dozen countries were killed, but the strain continues to pop up in Thailand, Cambodia, Hong Kong, and other places. The threat of a new flu virus arising for which humans have no immunity always exists.

Can We Outwit a Tricky Virus?

Prevent. Treat. Predict. Monitor. If we want to outwit a flu virus, these things need to be done quickly and around the globe. Can we do this?

Flu is passed along through coughing, sneezing, and

handshakes. One way to prevent a virus from finding a new host is to wash hands and keep them away from mouths, noses, and eyes. Another prevention is vaccination. Since scientists know that the virus is a parasite that can't reproduce without a living cell, they decided to make flu vaccines using fertilized chicken eggs, an old method. But the process takes months and won't keep up with a pandemic traveling around the world on jet planes. Also, vaccines are targeted toward specific H and N strains, and they only work until the flu virus changes its costume again. Vaccines will be much more effective when scientists can quickly create a vaccine that attacks the common structure of all flu viruses.

If flu can't be eliminated, can it be treated? Today there are antiviral medicines, like Tamiflu, that reduce symptoms and prevent the flu while people are taking them. But only a few million doses are stockpiled, and there are 6.6 billion people in the world. Most people will not have access to or be able to afford these drugs.

If the flu can't be globally treated, can outbreaks be monitored and then caught early? The Centers for Disease Control studies flu outbreaks in order to predict which flu viruses will be coming each season and to track unusual strains like H5N1. The World Health Organization gets information from 120 research stations in 82 countries in a global network to monitor contagious diseases. In Thailand, 900,000 volunteers make weekly bird counts and visit hospitals to inspect lung X-rays and blood tests. They do a great job of monitoring bird flu, but not every country is so careful.

If flu is discovered, a new FluChip that has been developed diagnoses the flu strain and origin by reading spots of genetic material dropped onto a microscopic slide. Some 5,000 subtypes of bird, pig, horse, and human flu can be accurately identified in less than 12 hours. A new redundant MChip is even better. Before this development, flu samples were frozen and sent thousands of miles to highly secure laboratories. Now if a new flu emerges from animals, it can be isolated and treated more quickly. Researchers are also looking for better ways to study the spread of disease. Lately they have been tracking dollar bills registered on the Web site http://www .wheresgeorge.com to trace how money, and therefore germs, travel around. In another study, Ian Davis at Ohio State University learned that young adults died so easily in 1918 because their strong immune systems attacked too hard. Their bodies, which would make fluid to clear the lungs, made too much and flooded the air sacs that supply oxygen to the rest of the body. The young adults didn't live long enough to fight off the virus because they couldn't breathe. This is leading to new areas to look for treatment.

To outwit the tricky flu virus, we must look everywhere and do everything possible. Influenza is not just a bad cold. It is a family of diseases that can be mild or deadly. The world will be better prepared for a deadly pandemic by understanding what occurred in 1918. "We definitely have the right suspect," says Jeffery Taubenberger. "We do not yet know how the murder was committed."

CHAPTER EIGHT

No Water, No Jobs, No Relief

The Dust Bowl of the 1930s

Borrowed Money, Big Problems

In the early 1900s, Americans learned to make products very fast. Henry Ford developed a car-making assembly line where "the man who puts in a bolt does not put on the nut; the man who puts on the nut does not tighten it." By 1914, this method of each person doing one small job over and over again resulted in building a Model T Ford in just 93 minutes. Millions of people bought cars for the first time, and the demand for gas, rubber, and steel multiplied. Interstate highways, service stations, and motels boomed. Other factories followed the assembly-line method, and soon refrigerators, washing machines, clothing, and many other items were in speedy production.

This led to a dilemma. Workers wanted the products, but they didn't earn enough money to buy them. In 1927, Henry Ford earned $14 million, but his workers averaged only $1,000. How could they pay for these fancy items hot off the assembly line? A new concept emerged: "Buy now, pay later." A farmer could borrow $5,000 for the latest tractor and pay it back at $35 a month. This payment included interest, which is an extra fee paid to buy something on credit. A city worker could borrow for a car, washing machine, or toilet, and then pay it back a little at a time. They went into debt. Sometimes people bought more than they could ever repay, and they could not get out of debt. Eventually far too many items were rushed off assembly lines for the number of people willing or able to purchase them.

Some people decided to make their fortune by buying stocks in the companies making all these products. Stock purchases allowed them to become part owners who hoped to share in the profits. They borrowed money to buy stocks in big companies like U.S. Steel and Montgomery Ward, the thriving mail-order business started up in Chicago after the Great Fire. Soon, with an oversupply of goods and far too many people in debt, the system developed problems.

Then, in 1929, the value of stocks began to drop. Montgomery Ward and U.S. Steel dropped by about $50 in September. Over the next six weeks, other stocks plunged in value too, and the phone lines and ticker tapes that tracked stock sales couldn't keep up with the changes. People panicked—everybody wanted to sell their stock before they lost even more money. On October 29, 1929, a terrible day called "Black Tuesday," the value of the stock market crashed. People lost billions of dollars.

This was the beginning of what is now called the Great Depression. During this first year of Herbert Hoover's presidency, one in five had no jobs, and the pay of those who still worked was greatly reduced. Banks failed. People lost their homes and bank savings and had no money to buy food and clothing. Children went to work to help. Around the cities, homeless people lived in shacks called "Hoovervilles," named after the president who did little to relieve the suffering. Recovery took years, and in the chaos most of the country didn't notice the situation on the plains of the Midwest, where crops were failing, cattle were dying, and people were sick and dying too.

Then, on May 10, 1934, a monstrous dust cloud (1,500 miles long, 900 miles across, and 2 miles high) dumped 12 million tons of soil on Chicago. The roiling dirt that should have been nourishing wheat out in the plains kept moving east. The black blizzard darkened Atlanta and blocked out the sun over Washington, D.C. People could taste the fresh soil that hung for five hours like a heavy fog over Manhattan. Eventually, ships 300 miles out at sea were covered in the dust that reminded one captain of sand from the Sahara. Now everyone was asking, What's the story behind this nightmare cloud of dust?

*Garden City, Kansas, just
before a huge dust storm
in 1935.*

*Garden City, Kansas,
15 minutes later as the
dust storm blotted out
the sun and the
streetlights glowed
in the sudden darkness.*

The Sodbusters

The dust came from farms in the Great Plains, mainly in Kansas, Oklahoma, Colorado, New Mexico, and Texas, as well as other states. Over the centuries, in spite of wind and many droughts, these areas had flourished, supporting bison, coyotes, rattlesnakes, prairie dogs, rabbits, sagebrush, and native grasses like bluestem, grama, and buffalo grass. Certain grasses were more abundant in rain cycles; others dominated during a drought, and these did a good job of holding soil particles and moisture in their roots.

Some of this land had been granted to Native Americans under various treaties, including the 1828 Treaty of Washington, in which the government promised a "perpetual Indian reserve . . . a permanent home . . . which shall, under the most solemn guarantee of the United States, be and remain theirs forever." The government, hunters, miners, settlers, and the railroads soon ignored these treaties. After the Homestead Act of 1862, ranchers, settlers, and land speculators sometimes lined up at the borders of what was supposed to be Indian territory and stampeded across the Great Plains to claim land in the middle of the country. The railroads controlled the best acreage and sold it to those who had money or could borrow it. Other settlers spread out into less desirable areas, where they could have land for free if they stayed for five years and plowed up a portion.

As settlers displaced the Great Plains Indians, there were many conflicts. Bison, the main source of food, tools, and tepee skins for the Oglala, Cheyenne, Pawnee, and other tribes, were slaughtered by the millions until fewer than a thousand remained. It took just 10 years to empty the plains of bison and Indians to make room for what General Philip Sheridan called the "speckled cattle and the festive cowboy . . . forerunner of an advanced civilization."

Newcomers lived on the land very differently from the Native Americans. Ranchers killed off wolves, coyotes, and prairie dogs. They kept sheep and cattle, not the bison that were always on the move to avoid wolf and Indian predators. These new herds were fenced behind barbed wire and often stayed too long in one place, trampling water holes and over-grazing the grass. The farmers broke up the sod, the thick tufts of native grasses, and used the blocks to make houses. They bought tractors on credit and plowed through the sod to plant crops. Windmills were constructed to pump up shallow groundwater.

Some people who were called "suitcase farmers"—

There were millions of bison and several varieties of native grasses thriving on the Great Plains before the farmers began plowing.

doctors, lawyers, and teachers from cities—came out for a few weeks every year, hoping to make huge profits on their crops. They applied the methods of Henry Ford to turn farming into a big production. During World War I, an extra 11 million acres were plowed up to grow wheat for Europe after the Turks cut off the grain supply coming from Russia.

The farmers were called sodbusters. The problem was that sod was the plant protecting the plains from the blistering sun and relentless wind. A rain cycle in the late 1920s brought prosperity, but then a drought cycle set in. Soil pulverized by the plow began to blow away. For eight years in the 1930s there was drought; more and more dust storms carried the rich fertility of the plains into the air. Crops withered. Ponds dried up. Wells turned to dust. Sand dunes covered roads and swallowed houses. Cattle starved. People coughed and coughed, and sometimes they died.

One of the worst days became known as Black Sunday. It was preceded by 49 dust storms in three months. Finally on April 14, 1935, the Sunday morning sky sparkled blue and clear. People used the rare sunny day to scoop dust out of their houses, bathe, and visit neighbors. But something wasn't right. Rabbits sprinted by, and birds screeched overhead, all heading south. Horses pawed at the ground, and cows paced. Hair stood on end, crackling with electricity that made the cars stop running. Blue sparks flashed along barbed-wire fences. Then a terrible wall of blackness blew in from the north. The dust blocked out the sun, and the temperature quickly dropped 50 degrees. Birds tumbled from the sky. People groped with their hands or followed fence lines or ditches, searching for shelter. In the oxygen-starved dust-filled darkness, lanterns wouldn't stay lit. Heavy loads of dirt from the storm caused houses to collapse and buried the roads. People and animals suffocated as dust clogged their mouths and noses. Some went blind in the thick grit that had "an edge like steel wool," reported Timothy Egan.

Black Sunday was one of the worst storms ever seen on the prairie. But people were familiar with so many others. Red clouds meant topsoil from Oklahoma. Brown clouds carried earth from western Kansas. Murky yellow dusters swirled up from Texas and New Mexico. Crops failed, schools closed, and tractors disappeared under sand dunes. Some farmers abandoned their land and struggled to take care of their families. Others waited hopefully for rain while they scrounged a meal of grasshoppers and canned tumbleweeds at tables smothered with dust.

The Gritty Nightmare of the "Dirty '30s"

Woody Guthrie, a folk singer, witnessed Black Sunday and wrote many songs about the Dust Bowl, including "So Long, It's Been Good to Know You" and "Dust Pneumonia Blues." The songs reflected some people's thoughts that the darkness was "like the end of the world" or that mid-America was turning into a great desert.

In Kansas, 12 straight days of dust storms destroyed nearly half of the wheat crop. Newly planted seeds blew right out of

the ground. Turning to other markets wasn't any better. One man tried to sell his hogs but could find no buyers because the animals were too thin. He spent $50 on feed to fatten them up and took them back to market. He was paid only $51.60. Ann Marie Low wrote, "My baby chickens are blowing to death. I've had to lock them in the calf shed for shelter."

Tenant farmers and sharecroppers didn't own farms but instead worked the land owned by others, usually the "suitcase farmers." As crops failed year after year, they were evicted and stranded on roadsides with few possessions. Millions of acres of pulverized soil were left bare and unattended.

Dust buried farms and equipment; killed humans, plants, and animals; and caused widespread misery during the Dust Bowl years.

In some places, people couldn't drink water or brush their teeth because of the dirt in it. Children got rickets and other diseases of malnutrition caused by lack of food. Nettie Featherston said, "We ate so many blackeye peas that I never wanted to see another one. We even slept on 'em, laid our pallets on the pods of blackeye peas and hay." On the other hand, many women took great pride in their ability to sew and cook, which reduced their monthly expenses. One housewife said, "We always bought bread, but now I bake and, oh, what satisfaction it is to turn flour, lard, salt, and yeast into crusty brown loaves." Mothers often gave a share of their food to the children. Ruby Sprague said, "When we were growing up, if Mother weighed one hundred pounds, she was fat."

Everyone was exhausted from the constant cleaning, which meant "scrubbing floors . . . washing all the woodwork and windows, washing the bedding, curtains, and towels, taking all the rugs and sofa pillows out to beat the dust out of them, cleaning closets and cupboards, dusting all the books and furniture, washing the mirrors and every dish and cooking utensil." And then doing it over again after the next duster.

The fine silicon particles—sand—caused a sickness similar to black lung disease in coal miners. The granules tore at the honeycombed web of air sacs in the lungs and started a disease called "dust pneumonia." The "dust hack" produced so much hard coughing that occasionally people broke ribs. Some died within days, and others suffered poor health for years. Sinusitis, bronchitis, and laryngitis were also huge problems, along with grit in the eyes. An unusually large number got appendicitis, perhaps from swallowing so much dirt. The Red Cross opened emergency hospitals and provided food, masks, nurses, and oxygen tents. They also helped with window caulking and other measures in an effort to keep out the dust.

Cattle suffered too. Tears turned to mud that sealed their eyes shut. The blinded animals then starved to death unless they breathed in so much dust that they died quickly of suffocation. An autopsy on a cow revealed a stomach so packed with soil that it blocked the passage of food. When crops failed, cattle were fed tumbleweeds salted or sprinkled with molasses. This did not provide enough nutrition, and they slowly starved. Calves born during a duster, which could last for five days, often died within 24 hours.

Snakes and birds died too, leaving grasshoppers without their predators, so the insect populations exploded. Millions of grasshoppers quickly chomped through any struggling crops, then "ate all the garden produce, even eating the cork out of the water jug left in the field," said a farmer. A child who forgot her doll outside discovered that the grasshoppers had eaten all of its clothes. Grasshoppers also ate broom bristles, horse halters, and clothes hanging on the line. They clogged car radiators and caused train wheels to slip on tracks slimed with their tiny, greasy bodies.

Rabbits, also without predators, multiplied quickly and became a problem as creatures on the plains scrambled for the last bits of food. On Sundays, frustrated farmers slaughtered rabbits that were eating the last of their crops. Up to

6,000 could be killed in an afternoon, far too many to butcher, and most of the meat was left to rot. Centipedes, black widow spiders, and tarantulas also became huge problems for the sodbusters as the creatures moved into their homes.

Throughout the "dirty '30s," everyone had plenty of time to discuss the situation. As they huddled in sod houses, Vaseline in noses, wet handkerchiefs over faces, kids covered with towels, water- or kerosene-sprayed sheets hanging to catch the particles, the sound of sand scouring paint from the barn, they talked about the dust, sometimes even with a bit of humor or the flavor of a tall tale.

Swirling Stories and Dusty Tales

- "Here is the test for wind speed in the Dust Bowl. Tie a chain to a tree. If the chain blows out straight, the day is calm. If it cracks like a whip, a heavy breeze is blowing. If it snaps to pieces and the tree comes out by the roots, a blizzard or twister is raging."
- "I hope it'll rain before the kids grow up. They ain't never seen none."
- "A man struck by a drop of water fainted, and it took two buckets of sand to revive him."
- "Now we get half a day between the Spring Dust Storms and the Summer Dust Storms, and then we get a day and a half between the Summer Dusts and the Fall Dusts."

- "Our locust grove which we cherished for so many years has become a small pile of fence posts."
- "Our last pig was a bit skinny. We ate everything but the squeal."
- "A sandstorm in which the flying particles do not achieve the size of small hen eggs is not a genuine Texas sandstorm but an imported variety."
- "For Sale—real genuine rainwater. This Kansas specimen has been specially imported and bottled in our own plant."
- "A Panhandle sandstorm will turn a chicken's feathers wrong side out quicker than a housewife can pluck it for dinner."
- "Nothin's worse than mixin' dust with a snowstorm. We call that a 'snuster.'"
- "The birds are flying backwards to keep the dust out of their eyes."
- "My dad used to walk the floor when those dust storms were blowing and say, "There's a lot of real estate exchanging hands today!""
- "My uncle will be along pretty soon. I just saw his farm go by."
- "You can predict a duster when the rattlesnakes start sneezing."
- "A number of signs signal the end of a drought. Of course, rain is one of them."
- "When you gits down to your last bean, your backbone and your navel shakes dice to see which gits it."

- "It's Russian Thistle Week. Eat your tumbleweeds—dry as cotton, prickly as cactus, and about as tasty as dirty twigs."

Go Home, Okie!

During the "dirty '30s," 40 million acres were ruined by the plow, and 9 million acres were abandoned. As one in four people left the Great Plains, it became the greatest migration in the history of the United States. They left from many states, but all of them were called Okies, referring to Oklahoma. It was not a kind term, for there were many prejudices against the people from the Dust Bowl. Signs were hung up that read OKIES AND DOGS NOT ALLOWED and OKIES GO HOME.

Thousands of the migrants headed to California, a place they considered to be the "Land of Milk and Honey." Some plugged along in old cars piled high with everything they owned

During the hard times of the 1930s, children across the country were supplied with milk by the Red Cross.

and a sign that read CALIFORNIA OR BUST. If they lacked money for food, lodging, gas, flat tires, and overheated engines, they stopped to work along the way. Some hitched rides in rail cars.

Crossing the border from Arizona into California was difficult. People who didn't have a job or a car were turned away. Migrants waited in long lines while border guards checked sacks piled on running boards and goods tied to the roof. They were looking for boll weevils, bedbugs, and fleas, and they turned Okies back in great numbers. For a while, the border was closed by 125 Los Angeles policemen known as the bum brigade. It was a rare time in history when one state refused to allow immigration from another. Eventually the bum brigade was called back.

Those who made it into California found few small farms, mainly large ones modernized into big production in keeping with the ideas of Henry Ford. Many became migrant workers, moving from place to place to pick grapes, cotton, and fruit. They earned 75 cents a day, maybe even $1.25 a day, if they were fast. They paid 25 cents to live in tarpaper shacks with no floor or plumbing. Some left farming altogether and looked for work in the cities, but it was still the Great Depression. After being offered a job for $17 a month, Harvey Taft said, "I can't. Less than a dollar a day, my family can't live. I know. I tried it too long." At the edge of cities, some lived in shantytowns called Okievilles, with no plumbing or electricity and plenty of polluted water. Typhoid, malaria, smallpox, and tuberculosis were rampant.

Migrants often lived in cars and trucks piled high with all their possessions.

Children went to work because they could be hired at lower wages. Most state child-labor laws were weak or unenforced. In 1930, there was no national child-labor law that applied equally to all children. Instead there were 2.2 million boys and girls ages 10 to 18 in factories, canneries, mines, and farms. Thousands under age 10 were also working.

FDR and the New Deal

In 1932, after winning all but six states, Franklin Delano Roosevelt was elected president. He took office the following March and immediately went to work on the problems facing the country. Calling his overall approach the New Deal, he started by insuring bank deposits so that people could trust the banks again. He set up many government programs, including the Works Progress Administration (WPA) and the Civilian Conservation Corps (CCC), that gave people jobs, dignity, and a source of income. The Social Security Act provided pensions so the elderly would not starve. The National Youth Administration, strongly supported by First Lady Eleanor Roosevelt, gave work to all needy students, black and white, boys and girls, so they could stay in school.

In a program called Operation Dust Bowl, the nation assumed a broader responsibility for soil conservation. A soil scientist named Hugh Bennett encouraged farmers to rest the soil, rotate crops, use contour plowing and furrows, and replant with grass seed from Africa. Some farmers resisted but followed the program when they were paid by the acre. CCC workers helped to clear sand dunes and tried to eliminate the grasshoppers. They also planted 220 million trees, from the top to the bottom of the Dust Bowl, to provide shelter from the wind.

The Great Depression got better but did not turn around until Germany invaded Poland in September 1939. Once again American products were needed to supply Europe in

A Civilian Conservation Corps worker plants trees for a windbreak to stop erosion. During World War II, most of these trees were removed in another great plow-up.

World War II. When Japan attacked Pearl Harbor on December 7, 1941, the United States entered the war too. Using new conservation methods, some Dust Bowlers were able to grow crops again, receive a good price, and pay off debts. Those who had moved to California found permanent jobs making ships and tanks. Workers from Mexico soon replaced them in great numbers to provide the labor on big farms.

Underground Ocean—the Ogallala Aquifer

The wind still blows across the Great Plains, and the cycles of rain and drought continue. The U.S. Forest Service replanted buffalo grass and maintains these restored grasslands in three national parks. But many did not learn the lessons of the Dust Bowl. In the 1940s, when a rain cycle returned and the demand for wheat increased in World War II, trees were removed to make way for another big plow-up. This led to new dust storms in the "Filthy '50s." Because some conservation measures were in place, this period wasn't quite as bad as before. Still, pulverized soil in the air caused car crashes and train wrecks, formed new sand dunes, and ruined millions of acres of wheat.

Farmers had always pinned their hopes on elusive rain, but sometimes it didn't fall when needed. So they started to create their own rain, using windmills to pull it up from a great subterranean ocean of water hundreds of feet below the area of the Dust Bowl called the Ogallala Aquifer. It filled up with water from melting glaciers about 15,000 years ago. In the 1930s, windmills could only pump from wells about 30 feet deep. But later inventions included strong pumps, aluminum pipes, and a quarter-mile-long circular sprinkler. These provided effective ways to mine this water from underground. It was called "liquid gold," and many thought it could never be used up.

Every plains creature depends on this underground source of water. As wells and pumps were added by the thousands, the water table was drastically lowered. Rivers and wells dried up. Runoff from pesticides, herbicides, insecticides, and fertilizers seeped in. In the great "pump-up" for irrigation and other uses, water was taken out eight times faster than it could be replaced by rivers in the Rocky Mountains.

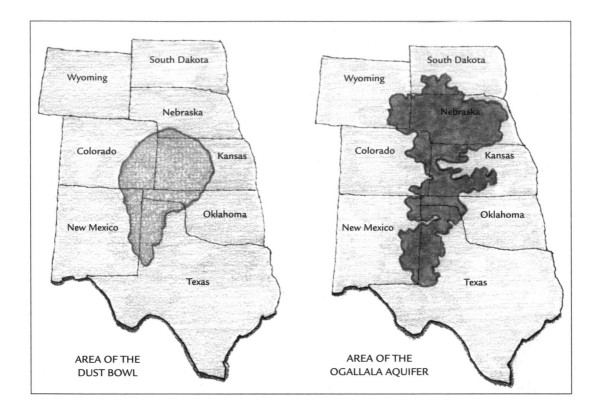

AREA OF THE
DUST BOWL

AREA OF THE
OGALLALA AQUIFER

The map on the left shows the main area of the Dust Bowl. The map on the right shows the main area of the Ogallala Aquifer, the underground ocean where farmers pump water.

Hugh Bennett, the soil scientist, reported that the dust storms of the 1930s were caused by the plowing of the grasslands. He also blamed the homesteading acts, which led settlers to plow up small amounts of land on acres unsuitable for farming. This resulted in "overcropping and overgrazing, and encouragement of a system of agriculture which could not be both permanent and prosperous." The plow-up of 100 million acres left 80 percent of the Great Plains negatively affected by erosion, and Bennett encouraged settlers to heal the land. But many continued to believe that drought was the problem and that the "rain" of irrigation sprinklers could solve it.

In 1977, the plains were in another drought cycle and experiencing great dust storms again. This time, photos taken from orbiting satellites were able to reveal that the source of the dust was West Texas farms, plowed and planted to seed, while neighboring New Mexico lands left in grass remained stable; dust was seen swirling up only from the plowed side of a fence. These camera shots showed definitively that land practices, and not drought, were responsible for the dust clouds.

In 2006, the Great Plains experienced yet another dusty drought, leaving farmers and ranchers without enough water to sustain their large operations. Many people are hoping for more conservation, more drought-resistant crops, more buffalo grass, and the rebuilding of bison herds. The plight of the plains is a serious challenge and something seen in arid lands around the world. How can we use water and soil now and still leave enough for future generations? How can we avoid dusters, snusters, and black blizzards that swirl away the soil from the middle of our country? The answers can be found in the lessons of the Dust Bowl.

CHAPTER NINE

Mammoth Shakes and Monster Waves, Destruction in 12 Countries

December 26, 2004

Head for the Hills! It's Earth Against Earth

For centuries, a big chunk of earth under the Indian Ocean known as the India plate has been scraping against another chunk of earth, the Burma plate. At eight o'clock in the morning on December 26, 2004, this scraping reached a breaking point near the island of Sumatra in Indonesia. A 750-mile section of earth snapped and popped up as a new 40-foot-high cliff. This created one of the biggest earthquakes ever, 9.2 to 9.3 on the Richter scale. At a hospital, oxygen tanks tumbled and beds lurched. At a mosque, the dome crashed to the floor. On the street, athletes running a race fell to the ground and a hotel crumbled. Houses on stilts swayed and collapsed. A man tried to grab a fence that jumped back and forth, up and down, and side to side. The quake, the longest ever recorded, lasted 10 minutes. Some islands rose up, and others sank, leaving "fish now swimming around in once idyllic, palm-fringed villages," wrote Madhusree Mukerjee. The shaking was so severe that it caused the entire planet to vibrate one half inch. And that was just the beginning.

Maslahuddin Daud, a fisherman, said, "I had barely started fishing when the earthquake struck. The earth shook violently, coconut trees crashed noisily against each other, and people fell down in prayer. . . . I lingered at the beach to talk with an older fisherman. We watched the water drain from the beach, exposing thousands of fish." He saw a huge wave filling the horizon. Someone yelled, *"Air laut naik"*—"The sea is coming"—but tourists stayed on the beach, and locals collected flopping fish stranded by the receding water. Few seemed to understand that destruction was rolling their way at the speed of a jetliner.

The Sea Is Coming?

All along the shorelines of a dozen countries, villagers, tourists, royalty, and soldiers were in the path of monster waves

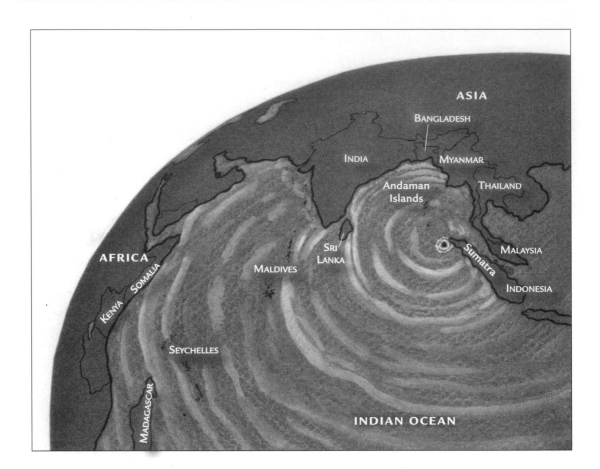

Racing at 500 miles per hour, the first wave took 20 minutes to reach Sumatra, 2 hours to Sri Lanka, 3½ hours to the Maldives, and 7½ hours to reach Africa. Traveling across the ocean at just two feet high, the waves piled up in shallow water to form great surges that reached 20 feet, 40 feet, and even much higher.

able to cross the entire ocean. People near the epicenter of the earthquake were swallowed up in less than 30 minutes. The tsunami didn't reach others for an hour, two hours, even six hours or more. Without a warning system, hundreds of thousands of people were caught unawares, many so far away from the source of the wave that they never even knew there had been an earthquake.

Yet earth against earth was the cause of all their

problems. When the sea floor ruptured, trillions of tons of water were instantly pushed up 40 feet by the rising land. Then the water came back down, and the collapse created a series of waves. These were not wind-whipped waves moving along at a few miles per hour. They were tsunami waves, racing out at 500 miles per hour. In deep water, the waves caused hardly a blip, but whenever one reached a coastline, the bottom slowed in the shallow water while the top kept coming, higher and higher, until massive walls of water, some over 100 feet high, smashed into land with the strength of many hurricanes.

The waves just kept coming, salty and polluted, with the second more powerful than the first, then the third and fourth, all so cluttered with debris that they became moving piles of concrete and cars, boats and coconuts, wood and tin, nails and glass, survivors and corpses. A shopkeeper said the noise was "like a thousand drums." As wave after wave smashed through villages, children were pulled from the arms of parents, clothing was ripped from bodies, and people and their possessions were flipped over, cut, and punched. Some were swept two miles inland, while others were caught in the backwash and carried out to sea. When the water started to drain, survivors shimmied down from coconut trees or other high places feeling dazed and confused. Weak voices called out to them from vast piles of debris. It was a changed world, soggy and broken; nothing looked familiar, nothing at all.

This was the scene in many countries around the Indian Ocean. The waves swamped the Aceh Province of Indonesia,

A boy scavenges for anything useful among the wreckage of a fishing town in Aceh Province after the tsunami.

surged through Sri Lanka, Thailand, Myanmar (Burma), Bangladesh, Malaysia, and India, flooded the Maldives and Seychelles, and eventually reached Africa. In Aceh, 169,000 died quickly, but death was also reported 16 hours and 5,300 miles away in South Africa. The tsunami left 225,000 dead, 500,000 injured, and millions without homes or jobs. One-third of the dead were children, and 9,000 were tourists. Plain luck helped some to survive. Only a few received a warning.

Trumpeting Elephants, Skittering Crabs, and the Power of Story

On a beach in Thailand, 10-year-old Tilly Smith was enjoying Christmas vacation and building sand castles with her sister. She noticed hundreds of tiny crabs scuttling out of the water. Then she saw the sea retreat far back into the ocean, like some great monster was slurping it up with a straw. No one seemed to notice, so she started to play again but then stood up in alarm as the sea turned white, churning with bubbles. A great wave was building up on the horizon as far as she could see. Fishermen's longboats were bobbing up and down like toys in a bathtub. Tilly remembered a geography lesson two weeks earlier at her school in England. These were the warning signs she had just learned. A tsunami was coming! Her mother wasn't convinced, but Tilly persuaded her father to get the hotel staff to evacuate guests while she alerted those on the beach. With this warning, they became some of the few survivors in the area.

On another beach, an eight-year-old named Amber Mason was riding on an elephant called Ning Nong. The elephant started to trumpet loudly and paw the ground with feet able to sense low vibrations. The mahout riding with her tried to calm the animal, but the elephant charged up a hill. While the girl, elephant, and mahout made it safely to high ground, others on the beach couldn't outrun the tsunami waves that soon followed.

Elephants and other animals pay close attention to natural warnings. They reacted quickly to the earthquake and tsunami.

Before the waves hit Sri Lanka, all the animals in a national park started to behave strangely. Monkeys chattered with terror, snakes went rigid, cattle bolted, and flamingos took flight. All of them scrambled to the highest places they could reach, and the keepers, who had never seen such behavior, decided to follow.

Near the Similan Islands off the western coast of Thailand, local divers saw dolphins jump madly around them and then torpedo far out to sea. "Quick, follow them," they urged the captain. They knew stories of animals that help and thought these dolphins could sense something unusual that the divers could not detect. Because, along with several other boats, they followed the dolphins to deep water, they were spared the smashing blow of the tsunami.

Closer to shore, Wimon, a fisherman, was eating watermelon when the strangeness began. The water turned murky with rocks bubbling at the top. He looked up to see the beach stretching out five times its normal width. Had there ever been such a low tide? Suddenly he was thrown off his bench and felt weightless. His boat bobbed up and down in a strange wave that surged past to flood his village to the tops of the coconut trees. He worried about his wife and two daughters, who couldn't swim. Then he saw the second wave, spitting, rising even higher than the first. Should he head straight into it? He watched other fishermen try, and their boats split apart. He decided to go sideways, was lifted 20 feet, 30 feet, until he was surrounded by a hazy mist and felt weightless again. He fell with a slam but survived. Of the 24 longboats in the area, his was the only one still intact.

The ancient tribes on the remote Andaman and Nicobar Islands have lived close to nature for centuries. They are said to detect changes by the smell of the wind and gauge the depth of the sea with the sounds of their oars. Every minute they pay close attention to the cries of birds and the behavior of animals. These natural clues warned them that something big was about to occur, and the stories of the forefathers told them what to do. "When the earth shakes, the sea will rise up onto the land. . . . Run to the hills or get into a boat and go far out to sea."

Some members of aboriginal groups survived the tsunami because they read the signs of nature; heeded ancient stories;

packed up their children, baskets, nets, arrows, and embers; and headed for the hills. Most people, however, lost their homes and precious possessions. Almost all wild animals, including tigers, elephants, water buffalo, monkeys, and birds, survived in good shape. Endangered orangutans and other creatures that live in the rain forests of Sumatra were not affected by the tsunami until it was all over. The trees are an easy source of timber, and forest creatures are losing vast acres of habitat as people rebuild.

Swamped and Scared

People caught in the tsunami suffered many injuries. After the waves receded, some were caught under deep piles of debris. A trapped deliveryman named Romi called and called for help but received no response. After two days, rain fell, and he was able to collect water for drinking. Mosquitoes feasted on him at night. On the third day, more people were trudging through the murky water to look for survivors. Four men tried to rescue Romi, but they failed. Finally on the fifth day, 25 men worked four hours and were finally able to haul him through miles of debris. All around, tens of thousands of corpses needed to be buried quickly. Elephants and bulldozers were brought in to help with the wreckage.

As survivors returned to their villages, they often found that nothing remained—no familiar landmarks, no driveway, car, or motorbike. The house was gone and everything in it, including toothbrush, comb, lipstick, and frying pan. Power was out, and phones were dead. According to one survivor, "Many people were literally left with nothing—not even coins in their pockets or clothes on their backs." They suffered from breathing problems after swallowing mud, sand, and toxic water. Before starting to rebuild, many spent days, and then weeks, looking for lost relatives.

On the first day, those nearest the earthquake were traumatized by 37 more tremors. During the next days, there were more earthquakes: 18 on Monday, 5 on Tuesday, 7 on Wednesday, 7 on Thursday, 9 on Friday. Each time the ground trembled, people who still had shelter scampered outside, "joining the others who feared that the walls and ceiling would fall in on them," wrote Barry Bearak.

The tsunami left a huge problem of contaminated water. In Sri Lanka, for instance, 40,000 wells were destroyed and the freshwater aquifer became toxic. In the Maldives, 16 coral reef atolls lost their freshwater and may be uninhabitable until decades of monsoons can refresh the supply. Other countries had similar problems as the salty waves mixed with freshwater and sewers. Thousands of banana, rice, and mango plantations were destroyed by thick layers of salty sludge. For drinking, Spain and Australia delivered gigantic water purifying machines. Military ships from the United States and Singapore made freshwater from the sea, and several companies sent water purifiers, including one that could turn raw sewage into drinking water in seconds. Some purifiers were lightweight and could be flown in by helicopter to areas that lost all road and bridge access.

Women serve food at a refugee camp in Sumatra, close to the epicenter of the earthquake.

As people sought help for severe injuries, supplies were scarce. At one hospital only 5 of 956 health workers were available. Barry Bearak wrote, "Little in the way of supplies was kept in the emergency room—no IVs, no pain killers, few bandages. As in many poor nations, new patients were examined and then their families were sent to buy drugs, syringes, and other items needed for treatment." When health workers ran out of anesthetic, ice cubes were used to deaden the pain.

When they ran out of suture threads, wounds were wrapped in plastic snipped from seat covers or left open. The ones who had wounds cleaned but not stitched were actually lucky. After three days, those with stitches often developed fatal infections when contaminated water was trapped inside their injury.

Relief workers from around the world eventually arrived with vaccines, antibiotics, food, blankets, tents, field hospitals, building supplies, and mosquito nets. In general, health care was well planned and prevented the outbreak of diseases, but the number of dead and wounded could be overwhelming. Sometimes tourists were treated before villagers. Villagers were treated before Burmese immigrant workers. Friends and family were treated before strangers. In India, people called Dalits, "untouchables," traditionally judged to be "less than human," were denied aid, even fresh drinking water. Social problems that exist before a disaster get magnified or changed afterward.

Rebuilding

Parts of India, Sri Lanka, and Indonesia were war zones before the tsunami, and these situations complicated relief efforts. In Indonesia, for instance, no foreigners had been allowed into Aceh Province for years because of the fighting. After so many died, however, foreign help was welcomed. Later, peace talks were held to aid the relief efforts because workers were afraid to go into war zones. Groups felt it was time for

Muslims, Hindus, Christians, and Buddhists to work together as members of a world community.

In many areas it was both the custom and law that women could enter the water only if fully clothed and wearing a head scarf. Therefore, most of them had never learned to swim, and the waves killed three times more women than men. Before the tsunami, women in Aceh Province had a hard time finding spouses because large numbers of men had died fighting in the long guerrilla war. After the tsunami, thousands of men were left without wives and children, and there were many new marriages.

In some areas, unscrupulous people saw a chance to increase their wealth during the chaos. A powerful corporation, the Far East Company, for instance, tried to take land from villagers in Laem Pom, Thailand, who had lived on a beautiful beach for many years. With all documents gone, it was hard to prove ownership of the land. A local woman named Dang decided to fight when the company posted a bodyguard to keep them out. Not only did the survivors want to rebuild, but they were desperate to search through the debris for bodies. Dang told her story to Parliament, but nothing changed. Finally she asked her neighbors to bring whatever documents they had; as a group, they would challenge the bodyguard. "He might be able to stop one of us, or even a few or us, but he can't stop all of us," she said. Twenty-seven families gathered together and were able to walk past the bodyguard. They set up a camp on a concrete slab.

An official offered Dang a bribe of five furnished houses

plus a scooter and telephone if she would leave. Dang refused and eventually received donations of 30,000 baht (about $830); 10,000 bricks; 5,000 tiles; and help from Thai students. Erich Krauss wrote, "It reminded her that there were still good people in this world—people whose hearts were large enough to care about the people of Laem Pom."

A man named Wichien missed the tsunami because he was inland diving for river sand used to make ceramics. His wife, Nang, tried to escape on a truck but got caught in a traffic jam. She had worked since the age of six and once learned how to harvest coconuts, so she was able to shimmy up a tree. She managed to hold on at the top even as ants swarmed over her body. As she called out to Buddha, she could hear what sounded like "a thousand children calling out for their parents and a thousand parents calling out for their children."

After spending several days in a hospital, she and her husband discovered that part of their house remained standing but needed much repair. Some materials were provided by a group who also brought Bibles and instructions to read certain sections. "Our God will help you," they said, and then sent a van to take them to church. This was confusing to Nang because, according to Erich Krauss, "She was a Buddhist. She loved going to the temple to pray with the monks. When the wave had taken her under, she had called out to the great Buddha."

The church group never really provided the help Nang wanted, so she took a job cleaning the house of a local official.

She then discovered "rice cookers, gas stoves, dishes, bowls" stored in a room instead of being distributed to villagers who needed them. When Nang asked for a rice cooker, "the leader's assistant would say she would get something tomorrow but the tomorrow they talked about never came," said Erich Krauss.

Wonderful assistance was donated to the tsunami survivors but many of them also had to deal with theft, deception, and disappointment. Relief workers had the best success when they found out what the local people needed, included them in the planning, and then made sure necessary materials were delivered. For example, when villagers wanted to rebuild using traditional methods, engineers gave them a demonstration showing that a similar but stronger house design would hold up better in the next earthquake. Models were made of both types of houses and put on a "shake table" to imitate an earthquake. When the traditional house crumbled and the reinforced house did not, all agreed the new design would be better. Then they worked together to include features that fit the lifestyle of the village.

Tree Zones

Many people noticed that some shorelines were damaged much more than others, even though they were close together. A study in October 2005 by seven nations that included ecologists, botanists, geographers, a forester, and a tsunami wave engineer found that "areas with trees suffered less destruction than areas without trees." They calculated that 30 trees per 100 square meters could reduce the maximum flow of the waves by more than 90 percent. "Just like the degradation of wetlands in Louisiana almost certainly increased Hurricane Katrina's destructive powers," they concluded, "the degradation of mangroves in India magnified the tsunami's destruction." They found similar results in areas where coral reefs had been destroyed to make shrimp farms. Houses with landscaping also experienced much less scouring and water damage.

After the study of beach damage, local communities decided to replant mangrove forests and clean out debris from coral reefs. These inexpensive actions will provide benefits not just for the villagers but also for sea creatures that use forest roots and coral for food, shelter, and nurseries.

In some areas, people have not been allowed to rebuild their homes along shorelines and must move inland. In crowded countries with little available land, this has not been easy. Fishermen suffered the most damage from the tsunami, and they prefer to live by the sea to watch their boats and nets. After the tsunami, some were sent to live in places so far from the sea that the transportation costs were more than their earnings as fishermen.

Warnings

The 2004 tsunami revealed that the Indian Ocean was in desperate need of a tsunami warning system, and 25 seismic

Tsunami waves can travel thousands of miles. They surge to tremendous heights when they hit shallow water, swamping everything in their path.

stations relaying information to 26 information centers were installed. Signs were also put up to identify evacuation routes. Still, the system is not yet perfect. Another earthquake and tsunami struck Indonesia on July 17, 2006, but warnings were not passed along in time, and another 600 people died. Some suggest that the loudspeakers used by mosques to call Muslims to prayer would be effective for broadcasting tsunami warnings.

The 2004 event also revealed that the Pacific Ocean warning system, in use since the 1960s, had only three of its six seafloor pressure sensors in working order. Money for upkeep had been scarce, even though tsunamis are common in the Pacific Ocean. In 1946 a tsunami started by an Alaska quake killed 159 people in Hilo, Hawaii, 3,000 miles away. Another Alaska quake in 1964 was a 9.2 magnitude, the biggest ever recorded in North America. It killed 115 people in Alaska, and the tsunami that followed killed another 16 people in Oregon and California. After the 2004 tsunami scare, the United States provided more funds to expand and update the warning system.

Nature may provide advance warning signs of earthquakes if we learn to read them. In underwater studies along fault lines, for instance, interesting changes have been found in the populations of single-celled microorganisms called foraminifera. These tiny creatures, with shells the size of a grain of sand, are very particular about their environment. When the elevation of land changes, the organisms relocate. In underwater earthquake areas, they seem to move about 5 to 10 years before the great shaking caused by uplifting plates. Scientists hope to learn more about this because it is possible that the foraminifera can provide warnings for disasters of huge proportions.

The "Orphan Tsunami"

It takes an underwater earthquake of magnitude 9.0 or above to generate big tsunami waves. Several events like this have already occurred on the West Coast of the United States, but few people have heard about them. The evidence has only

A mythic battle between a thunderbird and a whale is thought to describe an ancient earthquake and tsunami event in the Pacific Northwest.

recently been found, and much of it was not in places where scientists usually look. These mega events sometimes occurred when people with a written language were not around to record them.

The last event was over 300 years ago and has been called an "orphan tsunami" because some witnesses had no idea where it came from. The Samurai in Japan kept records of crop production for hundreds of years. On January 27, 1700, they recorded huge waves along 600 miles of coastline that caused flooded fields, ruined houses, fires, and shipwrecks. Since the Samurai were thousands of miles from the quake, they did not feel the shaking. To them, the big waves were a mysterious "high tide." Legends in Japan refer to this flooding event also.

Where did this orphan tsunami come from? Thousands of miles across the ocean, Native American myths in the Pacific Northwest provide a possible answer. Tribes from California and on up the coast to Vancouver Island have many stories that refer to a day when the earth shook and the ocean crashed, leaving villages wiped out and canoes stranded high in trees. Often the event is described as a battle between a great whale and a thunderbird. Makah elder Helma Ward said, "The tide came in and never left. There was a whale in the river and the people couldn't figure out how it got there." To pinpoint the date, scientists have found evidence of a magnitude-9 earthquake off the Washington coast that warped the seafloor on January 26, 1700. At the same time, a whole forest died just before the growing season began, and soil samples reveal great saltwater flooding in many coast areas.

The epicenter of this earthquake was just off the coast of Washington and Oregon, where the Juan de Fuca plate pushes under the North American plate in the same manner as the Burma and India plates. The next big earthquake here will threaten 10 million people along 500 miles of coastline that includes large cities like Seattle, Portland, San Francisco, and Vancouver, B.C. A warning system has been added off the West Coast and evacuation routes established. Scientists now monitor 24 hours a day and must live within five minutes of their work because some coastal areas could be swallowed up in 15 minutes, and every minute of advance warning will count.

The blend of myth and evidence found in the earth has brought scientists and Native Americans to share a new way of looking at the past called geomythology. Ancient stories tell us that events happened before and will happen again. Science studies the danger, while stories enrich the record and provide clues about frequency. Native Americans have developed a new interest too. Ron Brainard, chairman of the Coos Tribal Council in Coos Bay, Oregon, asked his mother to tell the stories again because before they didn't listen.

After the tsunami struck the coast of India, large carved rocks emerged from the sand. Some archaeologists say the rocks may have been buried since the seventh century and are part of the remains of a once-flourishing city that disappeared.

Now You See It, Now You Don't

In the disaster of 2004, coral beds rose up to become land, and several islands sank. These events were recorded by eye-witnesses, cameras, satellites, and other measuring devices. Sinking islands are more than myths. Six islands visited by early European explorers are now gone, some just under the waves.

In 1798, John Goldingham, a British astronomer and traveler to India, wrote down the details of a myth about the "Seven Pagodas," a group of temples from the seventh century that was swallowed up by the sea. The city was reported to be so beautiful that the gods sent a flood to engulf six of its seven temples.

That was the myth. Then came the 2004 tsunami, with ferocious waves that shifted great volumes of beach sand. This scouring revealed handmade blocks and carvings of a lion, the head of an elephant, and a horse in flight, all at the mythical location of the Seven Pagodas. Did the tsunami uncover an ancient mythical place? Archaeologists have dated the carvings to the seventh century and are busy studying.

Myths from the South Pacific also tell of deities that "fish up" islands from the water and sometimes throw them back. Ancient tales around the world are providing clues about other prehistoric seismic events. When it's earth against earth, nature keeps a record, and human survivors will always have a story to tell.

CHAPTER TEN

Hurricane Katrina and the Drowning of New Orleans

August 29, 2005

Sinking, Sinking, Sunk

For thousands of years, Native Americans lived in the swamps where the Mississippi River flows into the salty Gulf of Mexico. In 1718, the French made a claim on the land, and early settlers built a city called New Orleans on the natural high spots near the river. France sold the claim to the United States, and the city developed a colorful history of pirates and slavery, jazz and spicy seafood, steamboats and alligator-filled bayous. As more people arrived, homes spread out into the lowlands, built over squishy mud with sand and clay beneath.

Until about 100 years ago, the Mississippi River was wild and free-flowing. Water from thousands of streams and rivers tumbled into it with muddy sediments which eventually dropped out to become new land as the river slowed down around New Orleans. Many times the Mississippi flooded, piling up extra mud for the islands and marsh plants. The huge wetlands nourished alligators, snakes, and 350,000 migrating water birds, like spoonbills and pelicans. And they served as a nursery for much of the sea life that thrives in the Gulf.

Constant flooding, however, was a problem for people living in the area. They had to rebuild over and over again. A particularly nasty flood in 1927, all along the length of the river, killed hundreds and left 600,000 homeless. Like other cities along the river, New Orleans decided to construct high levees to contain and control the water. Millions of acres of forest were cut. Swamps were drained between the levees, and the city spread out into new dry areas. But, Al Naomi, senior project manager for the U.S. Army Corps of Engineers, explained, "When you take the water out of the swampy soils, they start sinking." Upstream, 1,300 dams were built, and the backwater behind them trapped much of the mud. Any remaining sediment was transported in canals right past the wetlands and out into the gulf. Without a muddy river to wash new sediments over the land, the sinking increased, and

Nutria are rodents brought from South America in the 1930s for their fur. Today, there are millions of them in Louisiana. Along with shipping lanes, canals, oil wells, fishing, lack of new sediment, and other causes, nutria play a role in the destruction of the wetlands.

most of New Orleans now sits in bowl-shaped terrain several feet below the level of the water around it.

Wetlands also were lost as 8,000 miles of canals were carved out for oil and gas companies, shipping, fishermen, and hunters. With global warming, water levels are rising, and islands are disappearing. More and more, freshwater areas are flooded with salty seawater that kills ancient cypress forests and marsh plants. Invading rodents called nutria are chomping down the remaining marsh grasses, roots and all.

These changes have turned the marshes into the fastest-sinking land in the world. This lost land once acted as speed bumps for hurricanes and the huge waves that come with them. As a result, when a hurricane came blasting across the coasts of Louisiana, Mississippi, and Alabama on August 29, 2005, so much land had been drowned by water that there wasn't much left to slow things down.

A Menacing Hurricane

It started out small, as a low-pressure area in the Atlantic Ocean. When it ramped up into a tropical storm, the weather service gave it a name, Katrina. It swirled up to become a Category 3 hurricane (winds from 111 to 130 miles per hour) and blasted across Florida, leaving nine people dead and a million without power. Then the storm reached the warm water in the Gulf of Mexico. Heat is fuel for a hurricane; it revved up to a Category 5 (winds over 155 miles per hour) in just 12 hours. The National Hurricane Center (NHC) put out an urgent warning: "Potentially Catastrophic Hurricane Katrina Menacing the Northern Gulf Coast."

Max Mayfield, head of the NHC, called officials at their homes to emphasize that this was the worst hurricane he had ever seen, and the area must be evacuated. Officials hesitated at first, but finally they ordered people to leave. Three million residents used all lanes of the freeways heading out of the lowlands. But not everyone left. Some didn't want to leave pets behind. Some had "hurricane fatigue"—they had

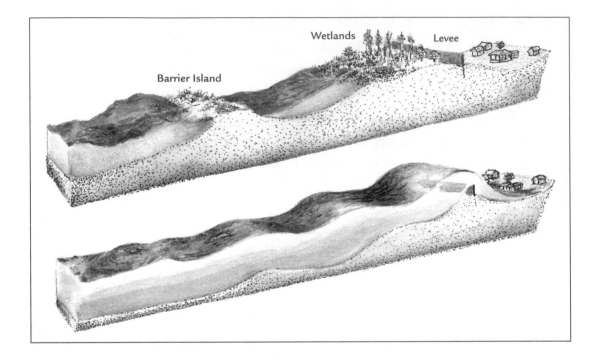

Barrier Island　Wetlands　Levee

Barrier islands, wetlands, and levees offer protection for a sunken city. When barrier islands and wetlands are lost, storm surge protection is also lost.

responded to evacuations in past years that ended up seeming expensive and unnecessary. Some trusted that the levees, the federal flood protection system, would protect them. Some were like Dyan "Mama D" French Cole, who preferred to sit on her porch in the Seventh Ward and watch Katrina come "crying, howling, like she lost all of her children." And many thousands of people in New Orleans were too poor or too sick or didn't have cars. They were stuck because buses and other transportation were not made available to them.

On August 29, 2005, the powerful hurricane raced across vast areas of open water that just thirty to forty years ago had been a healthy marsh and swamp. It pushed a great surge of water ahead of it. With marshlands gone that could have acted as buffers, and barrier islands sunk that could have slowed it, the wave reached the height of an ocean tsunami.

The hurricane slammed into hundreds of platforms used to pump oil and gas and then made landfall around 6 A.M. It splintered wood, tore off roofs, tossed fish, lifted a mobile home over a minivan, filled parking lots with boats, and blew tires, chairs, bikes, and cows up into trees. Julie Goodman reported, "You see it tear through your walls forming bubbles. . . . You hear the nails pop, one by one, off your shingles. You see water come through your light switches and drop down toward your bathroom sink."

The surge of water caused worse problems. Areas below New Orleans were walloped with a 30-foot wave and reduced to rubble. Waveland, Mississippi, a town of 7,000, was swamped by a 28-foot wall of water that destroyed 90 percent of the homes and businesses. Not expecting to live, people inked names and numbers on their arms for identification but then managed to survive by holding on to trees that were stripped of all leaves.

The hurricane slowed when it hit New Orleans. The storm surge was funneled into narrow canals and channels, which increased the pressure. The wind broke windows, knocked down trees and power lines, and shredded roofs, including that of the Superdome, home of the city's professional football team. By midmorning, the hurricane moved on, and everyone breathed a sigh of relief. The feeling lasted only until eyewitnesses began to report flooding from levee failures. Water was filling the Orleans East and St. Bernard Bowls of

This retaining wall failed, along with many other levees, allowing water to flood into the sunken city of New Orleans.

the city. A catastrophic breach sent a wall of water into the Lower Ninth Ward. Then the London Avenue Canal and the 17th Street Canal levees failed and flooded the Orleans Metro Bowl. Once the drowning of New Orleans began, it didn't stop until 80 percent of the city's neighborhoods were underwater, some by as much as 20 feet.

The Drowning of New Orleans

There was no warning system for the flooding, and people were caught by surprise. The healthy ones climbed to attics and rooftops or swam into the flood. Hundreds drowned, and thousands sloshed through murky water, headed for high ground as snakes and rats swirled into attics and alligators swam into kitchens. Many people headed to the Superdome, where some supplies were available but not nearly enough for the thousands who showed up. Without power, the water pressure was poor, toilets backed up, and air-conditioning failed at the stadium. When 25,000 people filled the Superdome, the National Guard closed the doors. A false rumor spread that the Convention Center, nine blocks away, was open, and 19,000 people ended up there with no lights, no food, no water, no toilets, and no security. Thousands more were on freeway high spots with no food or shelter at all. Only a few were able to escape in vehicles. The *Times-Picayune* employees, making reports until the last minute, finally sloshed through the floodwaters in newspaper delivery trucks.

There was water, water, everywhere but nothing good to drink. The floodwater became as toxic as a witch's brew. With 220,000 homes underwater, millions of tons of garbage bobbled around. Fluids leaked from 225,000 submerged cars and buses. Sewer microbes were in the mix, many times higher than safe levels. Bodies of people, cats, dogs, rodents, and fish added to the hideous stench that smelled like rotten eggs. Fumes rising from the water sometimes burst into flames. Clusters of floating fire ants stung people who got too close. Rescue workers, nurses, and waders all reported getting the "Katrina Rash" after splashing through the brew.

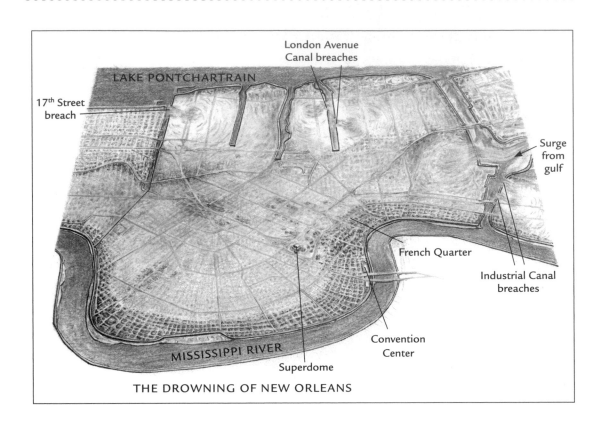

London Avenue
Canal breaches

LAKE PONTCHARTRAIN

17th Street
breach

Surge
from
gulf

French Quarter

Industrial Canal
breaches

Convention
Center

MISSISSIPPI RIVER

Superdome

THE DROWNING OF NEW ORLEANS

As levees failed around the sunken city, water flowed in to drown New Orleans.

Emergency help was needed everywhere. People hoping for rescue, including some in wheelchairs, were stranded on rooftops and in attics. But police cars were floating uselessly in flooded garages. Fire stations were underwater. Toppled power lines were blocking roads. Computers, cell towers, land phones, and even the 911 line were not working. Twenty-one hospitals and many nursing homes now had to care for thousands of fragile patients marooned without electricity. Hospital generators and fuel pumps were flooded, as were the huge pumps that could drain water from the city. There was an incredible need for freshwater, food, dry clothes, diapers, medicines, and medical attention, but far too little was available.

The Rescue Muddle and Red Tape Madness

Hurricanes allow for advance warning, and it is best to bring in supplies before the disaster begins. But before this hurricane, only 9 of 45 disaster medical teams had been sent to the area. According to Ivor van Heerden, head of the Louisiana State University Hurricane Center, the people in charge of relief operations "either didn't recognize how bad the flooding would be, or totally misunderstood what the impacts would be." Some were slow to face the problem directly, like Senator David Vitter, who said, "I don't want to alarm everybody that, you know, New Orleans is filling up like a bowl. That's simply not happening."

Michael Brown, the head of the Federal Emergency Management Agency (FEMA), waited until several hours after Katrina hit before requesting 1,000 Homeland Security employees to come to the Gulf Coast. He then gave them 48 hours to arrive. A medical team from the West Coast needed five days to cross the country. Help that was available was not always used. The USS *Bataan*, a navy ship with helicopters, doctors, operating rooms, 1,200 sailors, 600 hospital beds, and the ability to make 100,000 gallons of freshwater per day from saltwater followed the hurricane in and was ready to help. None of these resources was used except for the helicopters. The captain said, "We have to wait until the president authorizes us to do so." The Department of the Interior offered 300 trucks and 300 boats. The mayor of Chicago, Richard Daley, also offered hundreds of people and equipment. These resources were not used either. "I was shocked," said Daley.

Marsha Evans, the head of the American Red Cross, said, "Once the levees broke, [Homeland Security] didn't want us to set up Red Cross stands at the Superdome or, later, the Convention Center. They were trying to get people out of New Orleans." The Red Cross eventually provided relief across the United States to help people who were evacuated but gave no direct assistance in New Orleans.

Buses were finally located to evacuate people, but then it was hard to find drivers. Rescue operations were interrupted by reports of looting and gunfire, many of them false or exaggerated. When a physician from FEMA arrived at the Superdome, he said, "I've got a report of 200 bodies. The real total was six."

Some rescuers weren't allowed into New Orleans until requests came in for assistance. But how could people without working cell phones, landlines, and computers make requests? Some requests that came through were denied or ignored. Groups wanting to help often had to fill out papers and wait days for a response. This is called "red tape," and it is a maddening process when lives are at stake.

Rescue Relief

In spite of these delays, heroic and dangerous rescues started up almost as soon as the hurricane passed. Coast Guard helicopters were ready to go and pulled thousands of people from rooftops. The Louisiana Department of Wildlife and Fisheries used their marsh boats to ferry people from flooded homes and even evacuated 13 intensive-care patients from hospitals.

Ordinary folk and helpful neighbors came in dinghies, canoes, rafts, sloops, tubs, swamp boats, pirogues, air boats, and helicopters. They included a bartender, salesman, clerk, carpenter, reggae singer, and fishing guide. They endured the flying cockroaches and mosquitoes now swarming by the billions and didn't give much thought to tetanus or chemical burns. They saw a need and went to work.

Rules were strict, and all pets were left behind. Rescued people were usually dropped off on hot bridges and freeways. Some survivors waded to the Superdome or Convention Center while others waited, for hours or even days, for army truck transportation. After days of delayed rescue, some died of heat and dehydration. One woman said she survived by drinking mouthwash and eating toothpaste.

Once medical teams arrived, they controlled an outbreak of cholera and administered three million doses of vaccines. They set up a hospital at the airport and treated many patients although supplies were low and some slept on baggage carousels or behind car rental counters. Twelve thousand ill patients were finally evacuated from hospitals five days after the storm, but during this time, 215 died while waiting for rescue.

After five days with inadequate supplies in the Superdome

After a disaster, food is hard to find for both victims and rescuers. People rely on packaged meals developed for wartime. After the hurricane, the marines ate food called a tray ration, or "tray rat." It is similar to an MRE, or Meal-Ready-to-Eat, the preserved food eventually delivered to survivors stranded in New Orleans.

and Convention Center, thousands were transported by bus and plane to other cities. Some didn't know their destination until they arrived. Families were split up, and people lost contact with children, sick grandparents, cousins, and neighbors. Moving from one place to another, Katrina evacuees ended up in every corner of the United States, with the largest number going to Texas.

The rescue muddle was reported around the world, and donations were made in record amounts, with offers of help from 55 nations. But most everyone wondered, Wasn't this a disaster that came with a warning? Why did the rescue take so long?

The BIG ONE is coming!

In the history of the Gulf Coast, there have been many powerful and deadly hurricanes that have threatened New Orleans and other low-lying areas. In 1900, Galveston, Texas, an island city, was hit by a severe hurricane that killed at least 6,000 and destroyed most of the island. In those days, before TV and weather satellites, a warning came by telegraph from Cuba—this is a BIG ONE. This report was ignored in favor of local predictions, which turned out to be wrong. The hurricane was a Category 4 with a huge surge that caused the sea to rise four feet in four seconds. A 15-foot tide left the island submerged.

So many other hurricanes have hit the Gulf Coast that the area is called "Hurricane Alley." Many warnings had predicted a catastrophic disaster if a Category 4 or 5 made a direct hit on New Orleans. Hurricane Betsy caused levee breaches and flooding in 1965. In 1969, Hurricane Camille blasted away as a Category 5 with 200-mile-per-hour winds but veered east to miss New Orleans and destroy the Mississippi coast. In 1992, Hurricane Andrew ripped through Florida and then weakened. Still, it managed to tear holes in the levees protecting

New Orleans. Year after year, nature produced new hurricanes with advance warnings that someday, a big one would make a direct hit on the city.

For years, magazines, newspapers, books, and news shows added well-researched reports about the city's growing problems of sinking land and shrinking wetlands. These warnings came with such titles as "New Orleans Is Sinking," "Holding Back the Sea," "Gone with the Water," and "Bayou Farewell." In spite of this information, no plan was developed to correct the sinking situation.

In 2004, FEMA conducted a five-day practice run called "Hurricane Pam." The purpose of this exercise was to prepare for the possibility of a severe hurricane and surge that could drown New Orleans. A good plan was made to evacuate people with cars before a hurricane hit, but other plans, like taking care of people without cars or people in poor health, were left to be decided later and were never completed.

Warnings kept coming. Months before Katrina arrived, residents living near the 17th Street Canal levee reported soggy backyards. A muddy puddle grew into a pond that measured 75 feet long. City workers tested and found it to be levee water; drainage was seeping under the steel piling walls of the canal. No maintenance was performed then, but if it had been done, at least one neighborhood might have been spared a flooding disaster when the levee wall later collapsed in that area.

In a TV interview after the hurricane, President George W. Bush said, "I don't think anybody anticipated the breach of the levees." But 48 hours before Katrina struck, the White

House was presented with a slide show and a 41-page report that discussed breached levees, massive flooding, and major loss of homes. Warnings over many years, warnings right up to the last minute—none of them led to adequate planning for this disaster. Millions were affected by the flooding, rich and poor, black and white, Vietnamese and Native American, Latino and Cajun. Now that the bowls of the city were filled, with no drain plug to pull, something had to be done to remove all the water.

The Unwatering

The plan to deal with the drowning of New Orleans was to pump the water out. The Army Corps of Engineers, who built the levees, called this "unwatering." But it couldn't be started until the levees were repaired. While rescues continued, some helicopters were diverted to drop sandbags to fill the collapsed levees. Once this was done, a giant extension cord was used to power some of the pumps. Other pumps were added later. Gradually 30 billion gallons of toxic brew were pumped out of New Orleans and into Lake Pontchartrain. Some areas had to be pumped twice because another hurricane, Rita, blasted through in late September and flooded them again.

The unwatering took six weeks and revealed a city covered in black mold more toxic than the water. Household items left behind became health hazards. Volunteers went into homes in biohazard suits because black mold is capable of killing nerve cells and causing breathing problems. They were

The mold that quickly spread through wet houses was toxic. People wore masks and gloves for protection.

warned, "Whatever you do, do not open a refrigerator." Thousands of refrigerators were taped shut and hauled out to the streets.

A group of volunteers figured out how to use microorganisms to help with the cleanup: A spray of bacteria and yeast provided tiny microbes that gobbled up mold spores and then lived on the surfaces so mold couldn't regrow. They also planted sunflowers and mustard greens because their roots are able to remove toxins. Eventually, thousands of brick houses, clapboard shacks, and houses with great white columns on the front porch were cleaned, gutted, bulldozed, or maybe even rebuilt, if a lucky owner had enough money or insurance coverage.

Later, scientists discovered that Katrina was not the BIG ONE, a Category 5 hurricane, after all. It was not even a Category 4. According to the National Oceanic and Atmospheric Administration (NOAA), Katrina was a Category 3 when it made landfall and a fast-moving Category 1 when it passed over the city and Lake Pontchartrain. The drowning of New Orleans was actually caused by an "ordinary" hurricane. Levees failed because they were poorly designed, poorly built, and poorly maintained. No one wanted to hear that because it meant the BIG ONE was yet to come, and such a disaster had been created by a small storm. The amount of work and recovery left after Katrina was huge and overwhelming enough.

New Orleans Blues

An old blues song began to express the feelings of people who missed the culture and charm of their city—"Do You Know What It Means to Miss New Orleans?"

People who expected to return to the city in a few days instead found themselves homeless and jobless in strange cities. Some were desperate to find lost relatives and pets. Several Web sites were set up to help them.

Many people became involved in rescuing abondoned pets. They saved thousands of dogs and cats, five dolphins, and many birds, frogs, rabbits, and snakes. Evacuees traveled great distances to be reunited with their animals.

Cruise ships were brought in to provide extra housing, and service groups like AmeriCorps helped people adjust. They distributed mail, drove school buses, and provided day care and evening activities. Other volunteers nailed blue tarps over damaged roofs or went to work on the mold problem. Students showed up during school breaks to clean, rebuild, and help with frustrating insurance forms.

Thousands of evacuees moved into FEMA trailers, some in their own yards, others in camps. At night their tiny kitchens became bedrooms and couches became beds. After a year, some were still waiting for a trailer. FEMA had ordered

Wildlife is also affected after a disaster. This alligator ended up on a hot freeway.

200,000 after the storm, but the nation can produce only 6,000 a month. Many people discovered that insurance wouldn't pay to rebuild their houses because wind damage was covered but flood damage was not.

People hoping to return needed jobs, but 90 percent of the convention business for New Orleans canceled for 2006, and 175,000 jobs were lost. Few buses were running, and child care was rarely available. By February, however, the city was able to hold traditional Mardi Gras celebrations. In September, the Superdome was repaired and the New Orleans Saints football season sold out for the first time in history.

Ancient oak trees, toppled in the storm, were hauled to Connecticut and used to restore a historic sailing ship. Other historic parts of the Gulf Coast were forever lost, such as the Pleasant Reed House, built by a freed slave in 1887, and part of Beauvoir House, the home of Jefferson Davis, Confederate leader in the Civil War.

People needed medical care, but after a year, only 9 of 15 hospitals had been rebuilt. Lance Armstrong, a cyclist and cancer survivor, donated $500,000 for cancer patients whose treatments were delayed by Katrina.

After a year, some neighborhoods still did not have electricity or running water, and bodies continued to show up in the rubble. About 1,800 died in the storm, 1,600 of them from Louisiana. The 2006 New Orleans phone book was half the size of the 2005 edition, as 300,000 people had not returned.

Jason de Parle of the *New York Times* reported that some returning children were asked to draw a picture about their wishes for the city. Although they had colored crayons, they all drew in black and white, as if they knew their city wasn't yet back to a full, colorful life. Many adults were determined to rebuild. Those who suffered the most from destruction, disease, and death were black, nearly all of them poor. Hurricane Katrina had focused a spotlight on poverty in the United States.

Hurricane Katrina also spotlighted the Louisiana wetlands, the source of much of the nation's seafood, one-third of its domestic oil, and one-fourth of its natural gas. As New Orleans dried out and started to recover, many were aware that the wetlands were still there but drowning under too much water and starved for mud. Could they be restored as what Ivor van Heerden calls "the best, most natural, least expensive buffer available" for future hurricanes?

On June 1, 2006, the U.S. Army Corps of Engineers made a major first step by taking responsibility for the flooding of New Orleans. In issuing their report on the disaster, they recognized that the levees failed "because they were built in a disjointed fashion using outdated data." The old design did not account for sinking land and poor soil. The steel pilings were too short and unstable. As they develop new designs that include longer pilings and gates to allow for more flow of water and sediment, many hope that this will be part of a much broader effort to restore the wetlands.

One campaign was started with the slogan "Nutria: Good for you. Good for Louisiana." People are being encouraged to trap and eat the big rodents to reduce the population chomping through the wetlands. The meat, sometimes called ragondin, tastes like dark turkey. It is high in protein, with less fat than turkey, but so far not a major item on the menu.

Was Hurricane Katrina enough of a warning to make major changes? It will take plenty of time, commitment, and money to restore New Orleans. Yet many people do know what it means to miss New Orleans, and they are looking for the best ways to adapt, restore, and rebuild their lost community.

NOTES

Major sources for information cited in the text are listed by chapters in the bibliography. The names of all people in the text are real. For every chapter, numerous sources were used, including books, newspapers, magazines, Web sites, television documentaries, and photo searches at museums, the Library of Congress, NOAA, FEMA, and other online sites. Some of these references are highlighted below.

CHAPTER 1—Smallpox

Much information comes from the well-documented *Lies My Teacher Told Me* by James W. Loewen. The illustration for the sizes of various viruses is modeled after Figure 2.1 in *Viruses, Plagues, and History* by Michael B. A. Oldstone of the Viral/Immunobiology Laboratory at Scripps Research Institute. Quotes from Sir Jeffery Amherst to Colonel Henry Bouquet on colonial germ warfare can be found many places, including the Colonial Williamsburg site at www.history.org. The Modern History Sourcebook contains three original publications from 1798 by Edward Jenner on vaccination against smallpox: www.fordham.edu/halsall/mod/1798jenner-vacc.html.

CHAPTER 2—The Great Chicago Fire

The eyewitness account of Claire Innes can be found in *The Great Fire* by Jim Murphy. *Chicago: A Pictorial History* by Herman Kogan and Lloyd Wendt provided information for the early days. *The Great Fire: Chicago, 1871* by Herman Kogan and Robert Cromie is full of quotes, photos, and facts. The Chicago Historical Society, www.chicagohs.org, has additional photos and accounts.

CHAPTER 3—Johnstown Flood

Information about Victor Heiser comes from two sources: *An American Doctor's Odyssey* by Victor Heiser and *The Johnstown Flood* by David McCullough; quotes and facts on the flood are taken mainly from the David McCullough book. Further information can be found at the Johnstown Flood Museum, www.jaha.org/FloodMuseum/history.html.

CHAPTER 4—San Francisco Shaking

Many quotes and details come from *A Crack in the Edge of the World* by Simon Winchester. *Denial of Disaster* by Gladys Hansen and Emmet Condon represents two years of research in the National Archives to update facts, such as the number who perished and the attempt to suppress news about the earthquake.

CHAPTER 5—Triangle Shirtwaist Factory Fire

A main source is *The Triangle Fire* by Leon Stein. The Kheel Center at Cornell University also has much information at www.ilr.cornell.edu/trianglefire/. *Children of the Tenements* by Jacob Riis provided poignant stories about child labor, poverty, and struggle.

CHAPTER 6—*Titanic*

The complete 1911 report of the Immigration Commission on conditions of the Atlantic crossing can be found online at www.balchinstitute.org. The number and fate of passengers on the *Titanic* varies in different accounts; Encyclopedia Titanica, www.encyclopdia-titanica.org, was the final source for the figures because the site is highly recommended for accuracy and also provides photos and enough expanded information about the passengers to do a head count. The database of iceberg collisions kept by Brian T. Hill can be found at www.icedata.ca. Several quotes and details of food for the different classes of passengers come from *Last Dinner on the* Titanic by Rick Archbold and Dana McCauley.

CHAPTER 7—Blue Skin and Bloody Sputum

Much information comes from *The Great Influenza* by John M. Barry. Jeffery Taubenberger is quoted on the science from his own writings and other interviews. *Flu* by Gina Kolata has much information, including the adventure of tracking down frozen mummies to find the genes of the virus.

CHAPTER 8—No Water, No Jobs, No Relief

The Worst Hard Time by Timothy Egan is rich with details about the plow-up, the blow-up, and the aftermath. Documentary photos made during the 1930s and then 40 years later can be found in *Dust Bowl Descent* by Bill Ganzel.

CHATER 9—Mammoth Shakes and Monster Waves

The complete report by the World Wildlife Fund on surge protection from coastal vegetation, such as mangroves, can be found in the journal *Science Daily,* 28 October 2005, p. 643. The stories of Wimon, Dang, Wichien, and Nang come from *Wave of Destruction* by Erich Krauss. The details about Romi come from "The Day the Sea Came" by Barry Bearak.

CHAPTER 10—Hurricane Katrina and the Drowning of New Orleans

The Great Deluge by David Brinkley was the source for many quotes, along with *Come Hell or High Water* by Michael Eric Dyson. *The Storm* by Ivor van Heerden and Mike Bryan provided explanations, hurricane and breach research, and wetlands details that include a plan of action to restore them. Extensive information with quotes on preparedness, Hurricane Pam, the levees, evacuation, medical care, and other topics can be found in *A Failure of Initiative*; this 569-page final report can be found online at www.gpoaccess.gov/congress/index.html. A special thanks to Erin Halbert, AmeriCorps, and Captain Jason P. Smith, United States Marine Corps, for sharing their Katrina photos and experiences with me.

BIBLIOGRAPHY

CHAPTER 1—Smallpox

Desowitz, Robert S. *Who Gave Pinta to the Santa Maria?* New York: W. W. Norton, 1997.

Diamond, Jared. "The Arrow of Disease." *Discover* (October 1992): 64–73.

——. *Guns, Germs, and Steel: The Fates of Human Societies.* New York: W. W. Norton, 1998.

Ewald, Paul W. *Evolution of Infectious Disease.* New York: Oxford University Press, 1994.

Fenn, Elizabeth Anne. *Pox Americana: The Great Smallpox Epidemic of 1775–82.* New York: Hill and Wang, 2001.

Giblin, James Cross. *When Plague Strikes: Black Death, Smallpox, AIDS.* New York: HarperCollins, 1995.

Loewen, James W. *Lies My Teacher Told Me: Everything Your American History Textbook Got Wrong.* New York: The New Press, 1995.

Oldstone, Michael B. A. *Viruses, Plagues, and History.* Oxford, UK: Oxford University Press, 1998.

Peters, Stephanie True. *Epidemic! Smallpox in the New World.* New York: Benchmark, 2005.

Preston, Richard. "Demon in the Freezer." *New Yorker* (12 July 1999): 44–61.

Saffer, Barbara. *Diseases and Disorders: Smallpox.* San Diego: Lucent, 2003.

Townsend, John. *Pox, Pus and Plague: A Painful History of Medicine.* Chicago: Raintree, 2006.

Walters, Mark Jerome. *Six Modern Plagues and How We Are Causing Them.* Washington, DC: Island Press, 2003.

Watts, Sheldon. *Epidemics and History: Disease, Power and Imperialism.* New Haven, CT: Yale University Press, 1997.

CHAPTER 2—The Great Chicago Fire

Bales, Richard F. *The Great Chicago Fire and the Myth of Mrs. O'Leary's Cow.* Jefferson, NC: McFarland, 2002.

Ball, Jacqueline A. *Wildfire! The 1871 Peshtigo Firestorm.* New York: Bearport, 2005.

Chicago Historical Society. *The Great Chicago Fire.* Rand McNally, 1971.

Cromie, Robert. *The Great Chicago Fire.* Nashville, TN: Rutledge Hill Press, 1994.

King, David C. *Westward Expansion.* American Heritage American Voices. Hoboken, NJ: John Wiley, 2003.

Kogan, Herman, and Robert Cromie. *The Great Fire: Chicago, 1871.* New York: G. P. Putnam's Sons, 1971.

Kogan, Herman, and Lloyd Wendt. *Chicago: A Pictorial History.* New York: E. P. Dutton, 1958.

Marker, Sherry. *Plains Indian Wars.* New York: Facts on File, 1996.

Marx, Christy. *The Great Chicago Fire of 1871.* New York: Rosen, 2004.

Murphy, Jim. *The Great Fire.* New York: Scholastic, 1995.

Steinberg, Ellen FitzSimmons. *Irma: A Chicago Woman's Story, 1871–1966.* Iowa City: University of Iowa Press, 2004.

Warburton, Lois. *The Chicago Fire.* San Diego: Lucent, 1989.

CHAPTER 3—Johnstown Flood

Collier, Christopher, and James Lincoln Collier. *The Rise of Industry: 1860–1900.* New York: Benchmark Books, 2000.

Heiser, Victor. *An American Doctor's Odyssey: Adventures in Forty-Five Countries.* New York: W. W. Norton, 1936.

Kent, Zachary. *Andrew Carnegie: Steel King and Friend to Libraries.* Springfield, NJ: Enslow, 1999.

McCullough, David. *The Johnstown Flood.* New York: Simon and Schuster, 1968.

Ripley, Amanda, and Amanda Bower. "From Rags to Riches." *Time* (26 December 2005): 72–88.

CHAPTER 4—San Francisco Shaking

Behar, Michael. "When Earth Attacks!" *Popular Science* (May 2005): 46–60.

Bronson, William. *The Earth Shook, The Sky Burned: A Photographic Record of the 1906 San Francisco Earthquake and Fire.* San Francisco: Chronicle Books, 2006.

Brunelle, Lynn. *Earthquake! The 1906 San Francisco Nightmare.* New York: Bearport, 2005.

Chippendale, Lisa A. *The San Francisco Earthquake of 1906.* Philadelphia: Chelsea House, 2001.

Gaar, Greg, and Ryder W. Miller. *San Francisco: A Natural History.* Charleston, SC: Arcadia, 2006.

Hansen, Gladys, and Emmet Condon. *Denial of Disaster: The Untold Story and Photographs of the San Francisco Earthquake and Fire of 1906.* San Francisco: Cameron and Company, 1989.

Ketchum, Liza. *The Gold Rush.* Boston: Little, Brown, 1996.

Saul, Eric, and Don Denevi. *The Great San Francisco Earthquake and Fire, 1906.* Millbrae, CA: Celestial Arts, 1981.

Sherrow, Victoria. *San Francisco Earthquake, 1989: Death and Destruction.* Springfield, NJ: Enslow, 1998.

Sinnott, Susan. *Chinese Railroad Workers.* New York: Franklin Watts, 1994.

Wills, Charles A. *A Historical Album of California.* Brookfield, CT: Millbrook Press, 1994.

Winchester, Simon. *A Crack in the Edge of the World: America and the Great California Earthquake of 1906.* New York: HarperCollins, 2005.

CHAPTER 5—Triangle Shirtwaist Factory Fire

Altman, Linda Jacobs. *The Pullman Strike of 1894.* Brookfield, CT: Millbrook Press, 1994.

DeAngelis, Gina. *The Triangle Shirtwaist Company Fire of 1911.* Philadelphia: Chelsea House, 2001.

Freedman, Russell. *Kids at Work: Lewis Hine and the Crusade Against Child Labor.* New York: Clarion, 1994.

Gourley, Catherine. *Good Girl Work.* Brookfield, CT: Millbrook Press, 1999.

Kent, Zachary. *The Story of the Triangle Factory Fire.* Chicago: Children's Press, 1989.

Littlefield, Holly. *Fire at the Triangle Factory.* Minneapolis, MN: Carolrhoda, 1996.

Morrison, Joan, and Charlotte Fox Zabusky. *American Mosaic: The Immigrant Experience in the Words of Those Who Lived It.* New York: E. P. Dutton, 1980.

Riis, Jacob August. *Children of the Tenements.* Lifetime Library, 1971.

Schaefer, Adam R. *The Triangle Shirtwaist Factory Fire.* Milwaukee, WI: World Almanac Library, 2004.

Sherrow, Victoria. *The Triangle Factory Fire.* Brookfield, CT: Millbrook Press, 1995.

Stein, Leon, ed. *Out of the Sweatshop: The Struggle for Industrial Democracy.*
    New York: Quadrangle/New York Times Book Co., 1977.
Stein, Leon. *The Triangle Fire.* Philadelphia: Lippincott, 1962.
Watson, Bruce. *Bread and Roses: Mills, Migrants, and the Struggle for the*
    American Dream. New York: Viking, 2005.
Woodburn, Judith. *A Multicultural Portrait of Labor in America.* New York:
    Marshall Cavendish, 1994.

CHAPTER 6—*Titanic*

Archbold, Rick, and Dana McCauley. *Last Dinner on the* Titanic: *Menus*
    and Recipes from the Great Liner. Toronto, ON: Madison Press, 1997.
Ballard, Robert D. *The Discovery of the* Titanic. Toronto, ON: Madison
    Press, 1987.
Brewster, Hugh, and Laurie Coulter. *882½ Amazing Answers to Your*
    Questions About the Titanic. Toronto, ON: Madison Press, 1998.
Curtis, Wayne. "Titanic Ice." *Canadian Geographic* (March/April 2006):
    44–55.
Eaton, John P., and Charles A. Haas. Titanic: *Triumph and Tragedy.* New
    York: W. W. Norton, 1998.
Kentley, Eric. *Story of the* Titanic. New York: Dorling Kindersley, 2001.
Lord, Walter. *A Night to Remember.* New York: Henry Holt, 2005.
Lynch, Don. Titanic: *An Illustrated History.* New York: Hyperion, 1992.
Lynch, Don, and Ken Marschall. Titanic: *Ghosts of the Abyss.* Toronto, ON:
    Madison Press, 2003.
McCaughan, Michael. *The Birth of the* Titanic. Montreal, QC: McGill-
    Queen's University Press, 1998.
Osborne, Will, and Mary Pope Osborne. Titanic: *A Nonfiction Companion*
    to Tonight on the Titanic. New York: Random House, 2002.
Pellegrino, Charles. *Ghosts of the* Titanic. New York: HarperCollins, 2000.

CHAPTER 7—Blue Skin and Bloody Sputum

Appenzeller, Tim. "Tracking the Next Killer Flu." *National Geographic*
    (October 2005): 4–31.
Aronson, Virginia. *The Influenza Pandemic of 1918.* Philadelphia: Chelsea
    House, 2000.
Barry, John M. *The Great Influenza: The Epic Story of the Deadliest Plague in*
    History. New York: Penguin, 2004.
Caldwell, Emily. "Study: Fluid Buildup in Lungs Is Part of the Damage
    Done by the Flu." *Ohio State University Research News* (10 February
    2009).

Getz, David. *Purple Death: The Mysterious Flu of 1918*. New York: Henry Holt, 2000.

Kolata, Gina. *Flu: The Story of the Great Influenza Pandemic of 1918 and the Search for the Virus That Caused It*. New York: Farrar, Straus and Giroux, 1999.

"Influenza" *1918; The American Experience*. Robert Kenner Film, Boston: WGBH, 1998. Documentary.

Peters, Stephanie True. *Epidemic! The 1918 Influenza Pandemic*. New York: Marshall Cavendish Benchmark, 2005.

Porter, Katherine Anne. *Pale Horse, Pale Rider*. New York: Modern Library, 1998.

Ramen, Fred. *Influenza*. New York: Rosen, 2001.

Schaffhausen, Joanna. "Can Humans Develop Immunity to Bird Flu?" *ABC News* (14 February 2007).

Specter, Michael. "Nature's Bioterrorist." *New Yorker* (28 February 2005): 50–61.

Taubenberger, Jeffery K., Ann H. Reid, Raina M. Lourens, Ruixue Wang, Guozhong Jin, and Thomas G. Fanning. "Characterization of the 1918 Influenza Virus Polymerase Genes." *Nature* (6 October 2005): 889–893.

Taubenberger, Jeffery K., and David M. Morens. "1918 Influenza: The Mother of All Pandemics." *Emerging Infectious Diseases* (January 2006): 15–22.

Von Bubnoff, Andreas. "The 1918 Flu Virus Is Resurrected." *Nature* (6 October 2005): 794–795.

CHAPTER 8—No Water, No Jobs, No Relief

Ashworth, William. *Ogallala Blue: Water and Life on the High Plains*. New York: W. W. Norton, 2006.

Conrat, Maisie, and Richard Conrat. *The American Farm: A Photographic History*. San Francisco: California Historical Society, 1977.

Egan, Timothy. *The Worst Hard Time: The Untold Story of Those Who Survived the Great American Dust Bowl*. New York: Houghton Mifflin, 2006.

Freedman, Russell. *Children of the Great Depression*. New York: Clarion, 2005.

Ingram, Scott. *The Stock Market Crash of 1929*. Milwaukee, WI: World Almanac Library, 2005.

Gallant, Roy A. *Water: Our Precious Resource*. New York: Cavendish, 2003.

Ganzel, Bill. *Dust Bowl Descent*. Lincoln: University of Nebraska Press, 1984.

Hamilton, John. *Droughts*. Edina, MN: ABDO, 2006.

Hurt, R. Douglas. *The Dust Bowl: An Agricultural and Social History.* Chicago: Nelson-Hall, 1981.

Lookingbill, Brad D. *Dust Bowl, USA: Depression America and the Ecological Imagination, 1929–1941.* Athens: Ohio University Press, 2001.

Low, Ann Marie. *Dust Bowl Diary.* Lincoln: University of Nebraska Press, 1984.

O'Neal, Michael J. *America in the 1920s.* New York: Facts on File, 2006.

Opie, John. *Ogallala: Water for a Dry Land.* Lincoln, NE: University of Nebraska Press, 1993.

Porterfield, Jason. *The Homestead Act of 1862: A Primary Source History of the Settlement of the American Heartland in the Late 19th Century.* New York: Rosen, 2005.

Torr, James D., ed. *Westward Expansion.* Farmington Hills, MI: Greenhaven Press, 2003.

Woolf, Alex. *The Wall Street Crash: October 29, 1929.* Austin, TX: Raintree Steck-Vaughn, 2003.

Wunder, John R., Frances W. Kaye, and Vernon Carstensen, eds. *Americans View Their Dust Bowl Experience.* Niwot: University Press of Colorado, 1999.

Yancey, Diane. *Life During the Dust Bowl.* Farmington Hills, MI: Lucent, 2004.

CHAPTER 9—Mammoth Shakes and Monster Waves

Alverson, Keith. "Watching Over the World's Oceans." *Nature* (3 March 2005): 19–20.

Bearak, Barry. "The Day the Sea Came." *New York Times* (27 November 2005).

Boey, David. *Reaching Out: Operation Flying Eagle: SAF Humanitarian Assistance After the Tsunami.* Singapore: SNP International, 2005.

Bunnag, Tew. *After the Wave: Short Stories of Post Tsusnami on the Thai Andaman Coast.* Bangkok, Thailand: Post Publishing, 2005.

East-West Center. *After the Tsunami: Human Rights of Vulnerable Populations.* Berkeley, CA: UCLA Berkeley, 2005.

Krajick, Kevin. "Tracking Myth to Geological Reality." *Science* (4 November 2005): 762–764.

Krauss, Erich. *Wave of Destruction: The Stories of Four Families and History's Deadliest Tsunami.* Rodale, 2006.

Malaysia Medical Relief Society. *A Time to Heal.* Selangor Darul Ehsan, Malaysia: Writers' Publishing House, 2005.

Mukerjee, Madhusree. *Land of Naked People: Encounters with Stone Age Islanders.* Boston: Houghton Mifflin, 2003.

——. "The Scarred Earth." *Scientific American* (March 2005): 18–20.

Tesh, John, and Connie Sellecca. *Shades of Blue: The Tsunami Children's Relief Project.* Tyndale House, 2005.

Torres, John A. *Disaster in the Indian Ocean: Tsunami 2004.* Hockessin, DE: Mitchell Lane, 2005.

World Wildlife Fund. "Mangroves Shielded Communities Against Tsunami." *Science Daily* (28 October 2005). Web report.

CHAPTER 10—Hurricane Katrina and the Drowning of New Orleans

Audubon. Special issue: "America's River." (May/June 2006).

Baum, Dan. "Deluged." *New Yorker* (9 January 2006): 50–63.

Brinkley, Douglas. *The Great Deluge: Hurricane Katrina, New Orleans, and the Mississippi Gulf Coast.* New York: HarperCollins, 2006.

Carroll, Chris. "Hope in Hell." *National Geographic* (December 2005): 6–15.

CBS News. "Katrina Report Blames Levees." (1 June 2006). Television Broadcast.

Contreras, Joseph. "The Check's in the Mail." *Newsweek* (29 May 2006): 36–38.

Di Silvestro, Roger. "When Hurricanes Hit Habitat." *National Wildlife* (August/September 2006): 20–23.

Dyson, Michael Eric. *Come Hell or High Water: Hurricane Katrina and the Color of Disaster.* New York: Basic Books, 2006.

Ebeling, Ashlea. "Gambling on New Orleans." *Forbes* (19 June 2006): 93–95.

Editors. "Anatomy of a Disaster: 5 Days That Changed a Nation." *US News & World Report* (26 September 2005): 24–43.

Editors. "Debunking the Myths of Hurricane Katrina: A Special Report." *Popular Mechanics* (March 2006): 61–73.

Editors of *Time. Hurricane Katrina: The Storm That Changed America.* New York: Time, 2005.

Fischetti, Mark. "Protecting New Orleans." *Scientific American* (February 2006): 65–71.

Foster, Margaret. "Katrina's Wrath." *Preservation* (November/December 2005): 13–15.

Gulf Coast News. *Recovery News Report* (9 September 2006).

Hallowell, Christopher. *Holding Back the Sea: The Struggle for America's Natural Legacy on the Gulf Coast.* New York: HarperCollins, 2001.

Hayden, Thomas. "Super Storms: No End in Sight." *National Geographic* (August 2006): 66–77.

Hoffman, Carl. "The Kindness of Strangers." *Popular Mechanics* (December 2005): 86–91.

Horne, Jed. *Breach of Faith: Hurricane Katrina and the Near Death of a Great American City.* New York: Random House, 2006.

Kolbert, Elizabeth. "Watermark: Can Southern Louisiana Be Saved?" *New Yorker* (27 February 2006): 46–57.

Langfitt, Frank. "Residents Say Levee Leaked Months Before Katrina." NPR: 22 November 2005. Radio broadcast.

Lauber, Patricia. *Flood: Wrestling with the Mississippi.* Washington, DC: National Geographic, 1996.

Mulrine, Anna. "Freret Street Revisited." *US News & World Report* (4 September 2006): 38–44.

Moreno, Sylvia. "Tiny and Devastated Waveland Waits for Help." *Washington Post* (2 September 2005): A09.

Piazza, Tom. *Why New Orleans Matters.* New York: HarperCollins, 2005.

Streever, Bill. *Saving Louisiana? The Battle for Coastal Wetlands.* Jackson: University Press of Mississippi, 2001.

Tidwell, Mike. *Bayou Farewell.* New York: Random House, 2003.

United States House of Representatives. *A Failure of Initiative: Final Report of the Select Bipartisan Committee to Investigate the Preparation for and Response to Hurricane Katrina.* Washington, DC: U.S. Government Printing Office, 2006.

Van Heerden, Ivor, and Mike Bryan. *The Storm: What Went Wrong and Why During Hurricane Katrina—The Inside Story from One Louisiana Scientist.* New York: Viking, 2006.

INDEX

(Page references in *italic* refer to illustrations.)